101 WAYS
TO THRIVE IN A DIGITAL WORLD

TAÍNO BENDZ

Foreword by Hector Hughes

TECH-LIFE BALANCE

Text Copyright © 2023 Taíno Bendz

Library of Congress Cataloging-in-Publication
Data is available upon request.

ISBN: 978-1-57826-966-2

Printed in the United States

10 9 8 7 6 5 4 3 2 1

tech-life balance

also **tech/life balance** (noun)

using technology in a way that doesn't
have a negative effect on your personal
life or relationships

CONTENTS

IV

TECH-LIFE BALANCE FOR THE PLANET • 129

V

TECH-LIFE BALANCE FOR FAMILIES AND KIDS • 135

VI

TECH-LIFE BALANCE FOR SOCIAL LIFE & RELATIONSHIPS • 175

FOREWORD
BY HECTOR HUGHES

I T'S QUITE A TIME TO BE ALIVE.

Every so often, a new technology comes along that changes everything. Three to four thousand years ago, it was writing; pre-writing, all ideas lived in the mind. Civilizations prided themselves on their powers of reasoning and memory.

When writing came along, that changed. We no longer needed to hold all that information in our heads. This allowed people to build on the ideas of others like never before. It allowed them to gain a far deeper level of insight and understanding into a given problem. Writing changed the way we think.

But not everyone was onboard. Socrates, the great Greek philosopher, was a vocal critic: he saw writing as detrimental. To him, the written word meant the demise of memory. Without the need to remember, our minds would decay. To Socrates, oral dialogue honed virtue and developed critical thinking. All this was at risk.

Perhaps he was right; there's little doubt humanity has advanced wonderfully due to the written word, but at what cost? It's a tricky question to answer.

Now we find ourselves at the crossroads again.

Once more, new technology is revolutionizing the way we live and interact. At the time of writing, we're just 39 years into the internet and 15 into the iPhone. My gosh, what a change! Life is transforming at an unbelievable pace.

It's exciting. The digital revolution throws open a whole world of possibilities, nowhere more so than the smartphone.

We now have near-infinite knowledge and access to billions of people, all in a small device in our pockets. It empowers the individual like nothing else. Anyone with an internet connection can access a world of possibilities.

But it won't be without drawbacks. Attention spans are falling; stress and anxiety are rife, heightened by the constant stimulation; it's becoming easier to lose touch with the real and perhaps even ourselves.

So here we are. An exciting new world lies ahead, but at the time of writing we're ill-prepared to face it. There's no time like the present to learn how to thrive.

I can't think of a better guide for this than Taíno. He's thought long and deep on the topic so you don't have to. This book is the result.

All change starts somewhere. Much of it starts small: you might find the situation and present challenges overwhelming, but you shouldn't. Use this book as a reference. Try things, learn, and try again. I've found it a huge help in re-finding myself in the chaos of life today.

Socrates did not stop the written word and history barely remembers his warnings. But I bet he did some good in his day—because however transformative writing has been, we lost something. The same is surely true today. This does, however, present an opportunity: Get it right and you can have it all.

That's what this book can do for you. Take even a few of the lessons and, I promise you, you'll be happier and healthier for it. Start small, sure, but start. What you find may surprise you. Good luck.

—**Hector Hughes,** *co-founder of Unplugged*

INTRODUCTION

HAVE YOU EVER FELT ABSORBED BY YOUR phone and struggled to put it down? Been distracted at work, stressed out by the constant email or social media flurry? Are you a caregiver experiencing the challenges raising kids in a digital age?

If so, this book is for you!

You are not alone. We've got CEOs sitting in meetings absorbed by the emails on their laptop; parents pushing a swing with one hand while scrolling with the other; friends neglecting each other over their devices; kids struggling to play without the digital stimulation or shouting at their parents when asked to put the device down. I've been there, too.

But there *is* a better way.

"Dear Taíno, thank you so much for doing this. I have felt alone in my concerns about how technology is taking over our lives. I have a Paper Tiger Catamaran that I built from scratch. I have decided to call it "Offline" and race it in an effort

> *to encourage more people to spend a little less time connecting with technology and spend a little more time connecting with people."*

It was March 2020, and I had just organized the first Phone Free Day, my non-profit initiative to drive the question of healthy smartphone use. While most of the feedback and reactions we received were overwhelmingly positive, there were also those who criticized me for being a technophobe. I got a few spiteful comments online and was unsure of how, even if, to continue.

That's when the email above popped into my inbox. Despite coming from a complete stranger, it restored my motivation and gave me the confirmation I needed to keep pressing forward.

As digital technology is becoming more and more integrated with our lives, it is also an ever-growing distraction. I believe that technology should improve life, not be a distraction from it. I wrote this book to support you so that your life, not the technology in it, plays the lead role. You will find useful practices regardless of whether you want to improve your focus and productivity, reduce stress, improve your wellbeing, or boost your relationships. You will learn about research, but most of all you will have the opportunity to improve your own situation and move towards tech-life balance. Be warned—this is not just an inspirational book; you will be invited to challenge yourself as we aim for practical outcomes that can significantly improve your life.

Technology has been around for a very long time, but in the last decades there has been a rapid acceleration in the innovation rate and digital technology has in a matter of years changed the entire way of life for many people. Around 60% of the global population now has internet access, and as many as 95% in more penetrated markets. In the minutes since you started reading, we have collectively around the world sent around 180 million emails; tweeted 580,000 tweets; made 6 million Google searches; watched around 5.5 million YouTube videos and scrolled a distance of halfway to the moon.

I want to invite you on a journey towards using technology in a way that doesn't have a negative effect on your life. However, I do not think it is fair to you, or the technology, only to avoid its negative effects. I want to show you how you can *improve* many aspects of your life by shifting habits. I also want to add to the discussion around the development of technology and in which direction we want the advancements to go. Writing about technology that changes so quickly is hard. To avoid the book being outdated before it is even printed, we will be focusing on you. The one constant parameter in a swiftly changing world is the human at the center of it all; how we choose to use the technology, and why.

This book starts by looking at why some technology is so addictive and how we got here. We then look at how to build new habits before going into the six main parts. Each part addresses a specific area where technology affects us, and starts with an examination of research, followed by a plunge into an array of practical habits to support that particular area. To make it more real and relatable, many of these practices have also been tried out by people just like you who share their experience. To get the most out of the book, you will join me in the reflections and try some of the practices. Some of these will be known to you, and you might already be practicing them, but I am pretty sure that there will be something new for everyone! It will also help you discover some aspects that you have not considered that are affecting your tech-life balance and ultimately your life.

Balance is not a permanent state, it is not static. Your middle ground will change over time, and in addition you will sway on both sides of tech-life balance, sometimes using tech too much, and sometimes perhaps too little which may have negative consequences, too. It is also highly individual, and what is balance for one person might not fit at all for someone else. With this book you will be aware of what balance means for you, when you are not in balance, and get the tools to move back towards it.

I encourage you to reflect from your own perspective to learn what is relevant for you, and to discuss with your friends and family. I would suggest you get a notebook to write down your thoughts and answers to the reflective questions, and to follow your progress. Needless to say, the more actively you participate, the more aware you will become of your current situation;

of where you want to head and of the changes that will make the most difference for you in your pursuit of tech-life balance and time well spent.

> *"There's a myth that time is money. In fact, time is more precious than money. It's a nonrenewable resource. Once you've spent it, and if you've spent it badly, it's gone forever."*
> —NEIL FIORE, author of *The Now Habit.*

We have limited time and attention in our lives. I want to help you reflect on where you want to spend it, and give you tools to direct it where you want instead of letting the most absorbing video, loudest ping or brightest icon grab it.

So, where are you *actually* spending your precious time and attention?

PREPARING FOR IMPROVEMENT

Your Tech-Life Inventory

First things first. Have you ever taken the time to really evaluate how much time you spend in front of your screens?

> *"I believe that one of the most valuable things you can give yourself is time. Taking time to be more fully present."*
> —OPRAH WINFREY

Take a moment now to measure just how much you use your different devices. Estimate how much you use a computer for work/studies. Check the stats on your phone to see how many hours you spend on it, as well as how often you pick it up; Google it if you are unsure how to. And don't forget to add how much additional screen time you get from other devices such as a tablet or TV!

Grab a notebook and write down your total daily use across all devices, broken down like this:

Work/studies: _____ hours.

Leisure: _____ hours.

Of course, screen time (or device time) is not the *most* telling measurement—it doesn't take into account *what* we're using the devices for. However, it does give us an idea of the total time that we, in part, could be spending on doing something else—and who hasn't wanted more time for the important things in our lives?

Now, looking at those numbers, reflect on how they make you *feel*. Did seeing your screen time broken down leave you pleasantly surprised? Perhaps you thought it would be higher. Or perhaps you were shocked at the amount of time you spend on devices. Some of it may be necessary, e.g. for work, studies or communicating with people around us. But for many people, we go far beyond the essential and enter into the realm of dependency or even time wasting.

Remember these feelings as you work your way through this book. Each of the suggestions presented here is intended to help you find and maintain a healthy point of balance between on and off-screen time— specifically, one that works for *you*.

I have divided this book into six parts, each focusing on a way in which technology affects our lives:

1. Focus and productivity

2. Mental health

3. Physical health

4. Tech-planet impact

5. Families and kids

6. Social life & relationships

Each part follows the same format. First, we look to understand the problem through reviewing research on the subject. Then, once we understand how and *why* the challenge exists, we look for ways to address it. These suggested practices include self-exercises, tech hacks, reflections and more. Some practices are for you alone, some involve other people. They have been ranked in terms of difficulty from 1 to 3, with Level 1 practices being typically easy to do with a low entry barrier, and Level 3 serving as more difficult habit changes, reflections, or practices that may need to involve other people.

I encourage you to start with a few practices, or even just one, and stick to them for a few weeks at least. Reflect on why you are doing them, how they affect you and whether you notice any change. I don't expect anyone to try all the practices in the book—instead, consider it an à la carte menu where you pick the combination that is most suitable for you. Don't take on too much; I don't want you to feel overwhelmed! Giving up is fine, as long as it stems from an active choice saying, "This practice did not suit me."

For the best result, keep a notebook nearby to jot down your thoughts. These notes are great to come back to later along the journey to help you see how far you have come. I also encourage you to write down which practices you choose to try, the date when you started, what happened, and how it felt.

Remember that change is hard and reducing the stimuli from time spent on devices means having more time for reflection and looking inwards. While beneficial in the long run, it can be uncomfortable at first, but be proud of yourself and be kind to yourself—you are doing great! There is so much value in only having read this far and starting your journey towards a more conscious and balanced technology use.

First, let's examine how things got to this point.

How Did We Get Here?

When we say we want to strike a balance with the technology in our lives, what does that mean? Just what is considered "technology"?

Technology can broadly be defined as: "The application of scientific knowledge to the practical aims of human life." Note the word *practical*; in other terms, through the accumulation of knowledge, we develop tools with the purpose of supporting us and simplifying our lives. From the first stone axe made nearly two million years ago to the newest top-of-the-line smart-phone, the impetus is the same: to make life easier.

So why does it feel like modern technology some-times does everything *but* make life easier?

Now, technology being as disruptive as it is helpful is nothing new: innovations such as the automobile or the telephone completely reshaped the world upon their introduction. But regardless of how revolutionary the technology, they were still *tools*—ones which we used to our benefit, with few negative impacts on our direct personal life or relationships with others.

Digital technology is a different beast altogether. Information technology—devices that generate, store, transfer and process data—stand out in our history as the only technology capable of completely grabbing our attention and competing with "analog life." Add this to the rapid rate of technological evolution and we have found ourselves in something approaching **innovation numbness**: we rarely get amazed at technology anymore in the way that we used to, meaning we accept new technology without really reflecting on whether it actu-ally *adds* any value to our lives—whether or not it really is a helpful tool.

> *"If something is a tool, it genuinely is just sitting there, waiting patiently. If something is not a tool it's demanding things from you. It's seducing you; it's manipulating you; it wants things from you. We've moved away from a tools-based technology environment, to an addiction and manipulation*

used technology environment. Social media isn't a tool waiting to be used. It has its own goals, and it has its own means of pursuing them by using your psychology against you."

—TRISTAN HARRIS, former Google design ethicist, technology ethicist, president and co-founder of the Center for Humane Technology.

Every new device that enters the market is an undeniable application of scientific knowledge, but does every new device support the practical aims of human life? Let us go back to that stone axe, innovated some millions of years ago: it enabled its user to perform a particular task in a way previously not practical, or perhaps not possible at all. The purpose of the tool was clear and so was its method of use and intended outcome. Digital technology, by contrast, can often have a vague purpose, and unintended side-effects. Just think of email: an industry essential which has made communication much more quick, easy, and efficient . . . and which now has many of us spending hours a day stressed and desperately trying to keep up with our inboxes.

Even though people have criticized new technology for centuries, not the least the TV and the radio, the first two decades of the 21st century mark the point when technology first started being increasingly used in ways that can be harmful to our personal lives and relationships with others.

Of course, not *all* digital technology brings with it these potentially detrimental effects or the risk of addiction. The real danger comes from what I will be referring to as **attention-grabbing technology, or AGT**: *digital information technology designed to grab and keep the users' attention.*

The prevalence of AGT is fueled by an attention economy, where time spent online on an app or platform is the new currency and companies will do anything to keep the users' attention. These business models involve users paying for content with their attention, time and data, often not considering that they are indeed paying for these services. They are paying with one of the most sought-after resources on Earth: time. That's why it's called "paying" attention in the first place.

> *"We're the product. Our attention is the product being sold to advertisers."*
> —Justin Rosenstein, former engineer at Facebook and Google, co-founder of Asana

AGT is distinguished by a combination of factors which, taken as a whole, is what makes its influence over us so significant. It is mobile, affordable, personalizable, and easy to use. Smartphones were around for a while before the masses started buying smartphones, for example, but these weren't yet AGT. Why? While these early devices were mobile, they were neither affordable, nor personalizable or easy to use.

In this book, we will focus on identifying and managing our use of and (as needed) avoiding AGT because I consider it to be the type of digital technology that is most affecting our wellbeing and culture on a global scale. Many of the practices revolve around creating friction, which might seem counterintuitive as we are accustomed to working to *remove* friction.

But we *need* this friction to help support us and our brains in balancing our use of AGT. And no wonder: our brains absolutely love AGT!

AGT: HOW DOES IT WORK?

WHY ARE ATTENTION-GRABBING TECHNOL-ogies so addictive?

The answer comes from how our brains function with regards to nerve cells receiving and sending messages, both within the brain and between the brain and the body. For the signals to be transmitted between one nerve cell and another, we need a chemical substance called a **neurotransmitter**. Our brains have a lot of different types of these, but the one we'll focus the most on is the all-important dopamine—what's widely known as the "feel-good" substance but is better understood as a "wanting-more" or "reward received" chemical. Dopamine gives a great (but short-lived) feeling of satisfaction. The brain releases dopamine during activities we think of as pleasurable: e.g., eating, exercising, having sex, consuming alcohol, etc. In fact, our brains are designed to reward us for certain activities.

Our brain—optimized through evolution for survival in environments with scarcity of food, information, and social contact—is constantly on the lookout for chances to satisfy these needs. Historically, dopamine has helped us steer our attention towards what gives us the best odds for survival. As our lives depended on scanning our surroundings to find food and shelter while avoiding dangers, dopamine was emitted to make us feel good when we focused on things that were new, surprising, colorful, or in motion.

But it does not stop there. To further motivate us to go out *looking* for necessities, our brains can also reward us *in advance* by increasing dopamine levels in expectation of what is to come. We get a feel-good hit when searching for new, unexpected things.

See where is this headed? 40,000 years later we still have the same brain, with the same built-in objectives and motivators. A brain that is still rewarding us for finding new and surprising things in our surroundings. But for most people, these objects are *not* scarce or hard to find; they're constantly available at our fingertips despite no longer being vital for our survival. Our brains release dopamine to email pop-ups, social interactions online, the posting of a picture and receiving feedback, watching videos, scrolling social media . . . all discoveries of new information, and often colorful, in motion, and surprising if you think about it. And since we get rewarded by the hunt, we even feel good endlessly scrolling because every now and then, we might see something new or unexpected.

Having constant access to something that makes us feel good might not sound like that big of a deal, but with frequent dopamine releases, our brains actually *adapt* to this new, heightened level of reward chemicals. After a release is over, the brain reacts by reducing the levels below the starting point. This means that the next release will not take us as high as previously. The result is that we get into a **loop** of needing more and more to feel the same, with potential long-term effects being difficulty finding that feeling of reward and satisfaction in anything, while also focusing all our energy and attention on activities that make us feel good in the moment.

If this sounds to you like a description of a drug addict looking for their next fix, you are not too far off the mark.

So, a question: How can we use dopamine-driven AGT while protecting our wellbeing *and* keeping our focus on what is important in our lives? Answering that question is the whole reason I wrote this book, but for a start, let's learn about the impacts of these technologies and how to adapt our behavior accordingly.

Exercise: Understand Your Own Situation

Which aspects of AGT do you find addictive? How is your current tech-life balance? Take time to go through each statement below and reflect on to which degree this is true for you. If you want, write down notes in your notebook.

- I tend to lose track of time when I'm on my devices.
- I feel the need to check my device right away if it vibrates or makes a sound.
- I get distracted by my devices when I'm with friends or family.
- I spend more time on social media than I'd like.
- I'll stay on my devices instead of going to sleep when I intend to.
- I feel like I'm missing something important if I don't check my phone.
- I feel pressured to be constantly available at work or privately.
- If I have a question I reach for my phone for an immediate answer.
- I feel overwhelmed by the number of unread emails I have.
- I get into conflicts with family members or friends about devices.

If you want to know more about dopamine and technology, have a look at the interviews with TJ Power on page 237 and Anna Tebelius Bodin on page 233.

Now that you have reflected on your current tech-life balance, let us have a look at how we can build new, sustainably healthy habits.

BUILDING AND BREAKING HABITS

YOU MIGHT HAVE HEARD THAT IT TAKES exactly 21 days to form a habit. That is, unfortunately, a misnomer. Research suggests that the average time needed to establish a new pattern of behavior is **66 days,** though it can be both longer and shorter.

In a study of close to 10,000 people between the ages of 15 and 64, four out of five who made changes to their digital habits saw improvements to their overall wellbeing. For those who did not experience a benefit, the main obstacle was difficulty in sticking with the changes. Sticking with a new habit is not only about willpower, it is also about setting yourself up for success. So, before we get into some of the healthy practices

I recommend, let's look at how you can set yourself up for success from the get-go!

Stack your habits. Look for patterns in your day and think about how you can add new practices to your existing habits by "stacking" them onto things that you already do. For example, let's say you set aside a set amount of time each morning to make coffee or tea. On top of that, you've been meaning to incorporate more active exercise into your day. Stacking in this instance could be as simple as doing 10 squats and 5 push-ups while you wait for your water to boil.

Make it obvious. Put a note up somewhere you frequent, e.g., the bathroom, the fridge or a door to remind you of your practice.

Make it easy. We are more likely to form new habits if we make it unintrusive. For example, if you want to start reading instead of scrolling in bed, put the book you want to read on your pillow. Conversely, if you want to break a habit, you can introduce obstacles, e.g., by deleting social media apps on your phone to force yourself to use a laptop to access it. To start her running habit, Wendy Wood, a research psychologist at the University of Southern California, began sleeping in her running clothes to make it easier to roll out of bed in the morning, slip on her running shoes and run!

Start small. To improve our digital wellbeing, we don't need to quit all social media or get rid of our smartphones. Even seemingly trivial changes like deleting apps, managing notifications, or taking a short walk outside have been shown to improve our wellbeing and focus. Having just 5 minutes unplugged, for example, could be the beginning of a life where you are less controlled by technology.

Create accountability by involving others in your habit changes. Device-free dinners as a family, tech-free time out in nature together with someone, set rules together at home and at work that everyone follows, and you reduce the burden of effort on any one person. Or simply tell someone about your new habit—thereby creating some healthy peer pressure and accountability!

Prepare. If you have decided on a device-free morning, set yourself up by checking the bus timetable, your meeting schedule, and the weather the evening before. Or, if you are having a social media-free day or weekend, make a post the day before informing people and letting them know how else to reach you.

Reward yourself. Rewards are an important part of habit formation. Some habits give an immediate reward while others take longer to show. It may help to build in some immediate rewards to help you form a new habit. Perhaps a device-free dinner means cooking the family's favorite dish; or maybe you and your friends get together and put in a dollar for every app you delete and spend it on a night out bowling.

Be consistent and do it every day. Habits take a long time to create, but they form faster when we do them more often.

Use your tech to manage your tech use. Sounds counter-intuitive? Since we have our phones with us pretty much 24/7, they are a great tool to help you use tech more consciously. Make use of the "screentime" report; set time limits on apps, set alarms or reminders to take a break from tech. There is so much you can do!

Have fun. Focus on what you are getting, not what you are giving up!

> *"You have to make a conscious effort to change habits, be mindful about your day and how you want to spend it. I mentally fast forward to the end of the day and imagine what I'll feel like if I've been productive vs. what I'll feel like if I've wasted a large chunk of the day procrastinating on my phone or letting myself be easily distracted by technology that doesn't serve what I'm trying to achieve that day. I know that one will leave me feeling accomplished, fulfilled and happy . . . the latter will leave*

me feeling frustrated at the wasted time and the build-up of work for the next day due to not using my time effectively."

—JOVITA, New Zealand, who tried out the practice Phone Free Desk

Reflection

How will you make sure that you follow through on a practice you decide to try?

I

TECH-LIFE BALANCE FOR FOCUS & PRODUCTIVITY

W E WORK MORE THAN EVER, BUT WE GET less done than ever before. We *feel* busy as we handle all the information coming our way; sending and receiving emails while simultaneously attending a meeting. We switch (seemingly) seamlessly between private information on chats and social media and work documents and communication. At 5pm, we are exhausted from having spent the whole day busying ourselves, but many are unsure of just what they have accomplished.

This feeling of busyness should not be mistaken for productivity. Not only can it be stressful operating in a constantly busy state, but research also shows it takes its toll on our productivity.

Deep Work and Shallow Work

Deep work is when you perform an activity with deep concentration that pushes your cognitive capabilities, and by doing so create new value and improve your skills. These efforts are hard to replicate; and to be able to do deep work, we need a distraction-free environment. For many people though, we spend far too much time on the other end of the scale, doing what is referred to as shallow work. This style of working is not cognitively demanding but is rather an execution of logical-type tasks that rarely create new value (although they may still be important). We often perform these tasks while we are distracted. Shallow work has its place, both because routine-type tasks need to be done and because we cannot spend our entire time doing deep work. The problem with too much shallow work is that we feel busy, maybe even stressed, but we rarely see any output reflecting our experienced effort.

Multitasking

Multitasking is a buzzword on steroids by this point, due to us having multiple screens around us, a huge number of communication channels, and entertainment 24/7 in our hands. When I started my career, multitasking was considered a very desirable skill and I often got the question in interviews about how well I could do it. Turns out, only about 2.5% of people are actually able to multitask for real. The rest of us are instead effectively *switching* between tasks, which makes our brains less efficient, introduces more mistakes, and drains our energy. When we try to multitask, we are also more likely to stay in a constant high alert mode with heightened heart rate.

Our efforts to multitask also take a toll on our creativity. Switching between tasks requires a lot of working memory (brain storage) which can take away from our ability to think creatively. It makes a lot of sense that when we are constantly switching between tasks and use a lot of our brain storage, we find it harder to let out mind relax and think new thoughts which is what usually leads to those "a-ha moments"

The Cost of Interruptions

While interruptions used to be a phone call or a chatty co-worker, they are now abundant in both frequency and nature through digital means . . . and the cost is significant. Gloria Mark, Professor at the University of California, Irvine, has conducted plenty of studies on this and related topics and found that it takes us on average 23 minutes and 15 seconds to get back to a task after an interruption (!). We generally compensate for interruptions by working faster, but by doing so we make ourselves more stressed and frustrated, while we experience increased time pressure and perceive work as demanding.

Further, we are not only facing external distractions. Professor Mark also found that almost half of the interruptions are self-inflicted; working on a task while opening a browser to check the news, or refreshing your email inbox, are examples of self-inflicted interruptions.

Think about it. You sit down to answer that difficult email or write that project plan you've been putting off. You start well, making slow progress on a complex task. But as the initial buzz and energy wear off, your attention wanders and you go onto another task, whether work-related or private. The reason for doing it will differ for everyone but may include seeking out instant gratification, a fear of failure, feelings of anxiety, stress, or a combination. In a study from 2016, participants checked their Facebook on average 21 times per day, and email on average 74 times. Every 'check' creates a break in our focus and results in a few minutes of task switching. Needless to say, a whole lot of time is wasted on self-inflicted interruptions!

The reason having multiple tasks and obligations active in our mind reduces performance is due to a concept known as 'attention residue,' which is where the brain keeps processes active on task 1 even though we've switched to task 2 and stopped working on task 1. No wonder it slows us down.

The median length of our attention on a computer screen is about 40 seconds. Some compare our modern way of working to playing ping pong with our brain capacity. By constantly directing our attention back and forth we waste energy and make it impossible to achieve flow and get into that important state of deep work. Because, unlike a ping pong ball, our brain takes some time to switch directions.

. . . . .

To summarize this chapter in a sentence: many people struggle to focus, find motivation and get tasks done, and technology plays a huge part in this. Luckily, there are plenty of practices to support your productivity and get you focused!

1

Manage Notifications

LEVEL 1

One of the easiest yet most impactful tricks to improve your focus is managing notifications. On any device really: phone, laptop, tablet, and wearable (more on this in hack #42). Identify which notifications add real value to your life and/or are necessary, and turn the rest off. Be sure to let family and friends know how they should contact you; they might get nervous if they are used to getting instant replies on certain channels and then you stop!

> *"Using your smartphone without notifications for a mere 24-hour period can noticeably improve your concentration, as well as reduce your stress levels."*
> —Carnegie Mellon University and Telefonica

Tip for Success

Many phone settings now have the option of different profiles where you can have different notifications come through depending on the profile, as well as grouping notifications together and showing at certain times.

I turned off all notifications on the lock screen, banners, sounds and badges with the exception of calls, texts or FB Messenger and reminders I had set for myself. I feel that I'm much less distracted and really notice when I'm with other people that have all sorts of notifications pinging and coming up on their screens or even worse, their watches! We really do become a slave to our phones if we don't take control of them!

—PHILIPPA, New Zealand, who tried out managing notifications

2

Device-Free Breaks
LEVEL 2

Whether you are studying, working in manual labor, or at a desk, breaks are essential to assimilate knowledge, give the brain a rest, allow the creation of new ideas, and much more. While scrolling on a device *feels* relaxing as it releases dopamine and might be a 'break' from other activities such as work, it is actually a way of inputting even more information into the brain. At a workplace, breaks are also a huge opportunity to form a collaborative and inclusive environment. Taking a break that's free of additional overload is a great way to improve memory, reduce stress, boost energy, improve wellbeing and creativity.

So, on your next break—let the device be! Maybe you can even get your co-workers to join you in some offline chill?

> *"We'd have a natural break between meetings if we were all on campus because we'd have to walk from one place to the next . . . I realize it's important to give myself that break from the screen. When I do that, I feel more focused during my next appointment."*
>
> —SHANNA FITZPATRICK, Chief Financial Officer Duke Graduate School

3

Phone-Free Desk
LEVEL 1

According to a 2016 productivity study by Kaspersky lab, removing the phone from your desk can improve your focus by 26 percent! This simple practice is a great way to break the attention-grabbing spell of your phone and only use it actively when you want/need to. Simply put it away out of sight after you have used it. And no, your pocket does not count!

Tips for Success

- Combine with the practice of managing notifications (hack #1) and keep sound on for any notifications you want to be alerted by (e.g., calls.)
- Have a designated place at work for your phone when not in use; e.g., a drawer or a bag.

4

Empty the Home Screen on Your Phone
LEVEL 1

Take all those shortcuts cluttering your home screen and get rid of them! By making it a little bit harder to use our apps, we introduce some much-needed friction that can support us in taking control and being more mindful of our phone use. Simply move all apps away from the home screen (the first screen when you unlock) and hide those you want to use the least the furthest away. The idea is to have nothing on the home screen so that when you unlock the phone you do not see any apps trying to grab your attention. For information on deleting apps, check out hack #28.

> *"Often you only open an app because it's there—this avoids that automatic, mindless checking. Plus sheer human laziness means you'll usually find the download-and-login faff more trouble than it's worth, which is perfect."*
>
> —MADELEINE HOLDEN, senior writer/editor "IRL" at The Spinoff on deleting apps

5

Turn Your Phone to Grayscale
LEVEL 2

Our brains are hardwired to get excited by anything bright and shiny. Colors are important to our understanding of priorities and emotions. Therefore, this simple trick can be more effective than you might think to make your phone less addictive. When apps, games, articles, lose their visual appeal, the phone is less fun to use, some of the positive reinforcement is removed, and it becomes easier to put it down and focus our attention on what we really want to do. Simply Google "greyscale" and your phone model to see how it is done! As a bonus—it improves battery life! It is also handy shortcut to quickly toggle greyscale on and off for when you want to consume content in color.

> *"I've been gray for a couple days, and it's remarkable how well it has eased my twitchy phone checking, suggesting that one way to break phone attachment may be to, essentially, make my phone a little worse. We're simple animals, excited by bright colors, it turns out."*
>
> —NICK BILTON, *New York Times* tech
> columnist, and self-diagnosed
> smartphone addict.

6

Phone-Free Meetings

LEVEL 2

Do this whether you're engaging in an online or in-person meeting for full focus on the meeting and the people in it. Ideally, this should be a policy for most organizations to adopt. If you feel the urge to pick up your phone when the meetings get boring or feel unnecessary, that is a great observation! Bring this up with your co-workers—they probably feel the same and you can have a productive discussion on the general meeting culture instead of wasting your time on your phones. Perhaps there are too many meetings, or they are too long? Or more people than those immediately affected are expected to attend?

> *"This challenge was a good prompt to reset how I use my phone. Having my phone out of sight during work time enabled me to better focus on my work and have a more productive day—therefore ending the day more fulfilled."*
>
> —JOVITA, New Zealand, who tried on phone-free desk and meetings

7

Single-Task

LEVEL 2

Single-tasking is the antidote to multitasking. Instead of constantly switching between tasks, wasting cognitive energy, and being busy yet unproductive, single-tasking is about giving each task the attention it deserves. This improves focus and productivity while reducing overall stress.

The next time you are working on a task, be conscious of when your mind is diverted from the task and try to bring your attention back. In the beginning, you might switch to another task without realizing it, but gradually you will start to notice and eventually you will work up the skill to be proactive and avoid letting your attention slip away in the first place.

However, keep in mind that a persistent urge to switch tasks might be a useful signal that you need a break and a healthy serotonin & endorphin kick by going outside!

8

Use the Pomodoro Technique for Focus

LEVEL 2

Timeboxing, i.e. dividing up your time and tasks into slots, can be a great way of both improving your productivity and forcing yourself into deep work. It is also a good way to actually get to those to-do tasks that you put off day after day.

The Pomodoro method—famously inspired by the Italian word for tomato from the tomato shaped kitchen timer—encourages time boxes of 25 minutes, each followed by a 5-minute break. This technique can be refined and there are also apps to enhance it further, but in its simplest version, you just set a timer for 25 minutes and get working! When the timer rings, take a 5-minute break away from any new input.

Using an app on the phone works well for this, but an online timer is even better as your phone can stay put away to avoid distractions.

Tips for Success

Think about what distracts you most when you are trying to focus. Is it notifications on the phone? Chatty co-workers? Family members? Procrastination? A constant stream of emails?

Instead of just accepting that you're going to be distracted, identify the major challenges that you face and work on reducing them by e.g. going somewhere quiet, using your phone's focus mode or turning off emails. Some even put up a physical sign above their desk saying Do Not Disturb!

Be sure to make your breaks tech-free to avoid overstimulating your brain with even more input.

9

Use the 5-Minute Technique

LEVEL 2

Used by Instagram's CEO Kevin Systrom and many more high profile people, this is simply a deal you make with yourself whenever faced with a task you either struggle to start with or which is constantly interrupted by procrastination.

The idea? Make a deal with yourself to commit to the task for 5 minutes *no matter what*. Set a timer and just start.

After five minutes are up, odds are that you are either done or have pushed yourself into a flow.

10

Timebox Your Email Use

LEVEL 2

Select a few dedicated time slots during your workday where you check and reply to emails. I do it twice: at 9am and 2pm, but some people will choose to have more slots. Or perhaps you reverse it and have access to emails all day *except* certain hours where you have dedicated focus mode. The important thing is to have some time during the day when you break the constant, stressful and distracting email connectivity.

Tips for Success

Communicate clearly so people know how to reach you for urgent matters. I have also found that once you stop responding straight away, you gradually change people's expectations of your responsiveness.

"...After spending five days off of email, the participants in the study reported feeling more in control of their work without constantly reading and responding to messages. They also found they had more time to complete work tasks."

—Los Angeles Times

11

Set Expectations With a Smart Email Signature

LEVEL 1

That little line at the end of your email is a great way to set clear expectations around your availability and choice of channels. If you are doing some of the other practices included in this book to balance your email use, such as setting specific time slots for responding to email, putting a short line about this in your email signature can really help.

This is what my own signature looks like beneath my name and details:

I work distraction-free during large parts of the day to maximize my focus and productivity. I normally check emails at 9 am and 2 pm. If your message requires immediate attention, please call me at XXX-XXXX.

12

Turn Email Notifications Off
LEVEL 2

Have you ever been distracted by that little pop-up envelope in the lower-right corner of your screen, or a ping on the phone saying you have a new email? For many people, email notifications are one of the major interruptions and stress factors. It's easy to think that we have to check an email as soon as we get it, but most of us don't (at least, not *really*).

This is a great way of taking back control of your time and checking your email when you want to and not when your laptop or phone tells you that you have a new message. Simply turn off the email notifications on your phone and laptop.

While scary at first, just know that the world does keep on spinning!

Tips for Success

If you think that colleagues or your boss would have a problem with this, point out that you do this to improve your productivity and focus! If there is still pushback, try discussing response expectations as an organization to make sure everyone is on the same page.

13

Clear Your Inbox
LEVEL 2

Full inboxes waste 27 minutes per day as a crowded inbox makes us re-reading emails over and over again. Emails in the inbox divert our attention and are a constant reminder of to-dos and unfinished tasks. Take some time and go through your inbox. You don't need to reach zero, but having it under control will give you a good feeling.

Tips for Success

- Archive or delete anything that does not need handling.
- Reply/handle smaller matters straight away.
- For each email that you cannot handle right now, designate a time in the calendar to do it (in Outlook you can even drag emails straight into the calendar and in Gmail you can do the same with a few clicks).

Depending on the state of your particular inbox, this can require setting aside a few hours, but the reward is worth it!

Unsubscribe from Unwanted Emails

LEVEL 1

I used to just click away newsletters/promo emails, but naturally they kept piling up. It wasn't until I decided to start unsubscribing instead that I realized the sheer *volume* of worthless emails I was receiving. I racked up a total of 74 unsubscribed email sources in the first week! Some emails were related to purchases I made 10 years ago. At a glance, this might not sound like a high-impact practice, but think about it: over a year, we get hundreds if not thousands of unwanted or irrelevant emails and if you spend a second to delete each, the time spent adds up—and adds to the distraction!

Every time you get a newsletter or promotional email, ask yourself: Do I read it? Do I need it? If the answer is no, then unsubscribe. You can always subscribe again.

Tips for Success

Some newsletters are as simple as a click while others are a bit more tricky. Don't give up!

15

Turn Off Self-View in Video Meetings
LEVEL 1

Imagine being in a meeting and being sat right in front of a mirror. The entire time, you constantly see yourself really close up. Are you focused on what's being discussed? Or are you distracted by how you look today and if your nose really is *that* big?

The huge upsurge in online meetings is taking its toll for many different reasons, and one super simple trick is to turn off your self-view. That way, others can still see you, but you do not need to see yourself constantly. Turning of your self-view may lower stress as well as increasing your focus and attention. Most video platforms have this functionality, so give it a go!

Did you know?

Plastic surgery is massively increasing as a result of millions of people working from home and spending hours looking at their own image in video calls. In the US alone, The American Academy of Facial Plastic and Reconstructive Surgery reckons that the Covid-19 pandemic has led to a 10% increase in cosmetic surgery countrywide

"Hiding your own display can give your brain some respite. You can turn your attention to what's being discussed."

—SCOTT KOLLINS, professor at
Duke University

16

Timebox Your Social Media Use
LEVEL 2

It is okay to enjoy social media. However, many people use it as a distraction, engaging with it mindlessly or aimlessly. Timeboxing social media not only reduces these distractions but it can even make your experience more enjoyable.

Choose a few times and places when you *are supposed to* and *allowed* to use social media. Set a timer and stop when the time is up.

> "*Scheduling my social media use definitely made me aware of how often I would just jump on my phone and start scrolling mindlessly. I also found it actually reduced the amount of time I spent on social media when I did go on, as it felt weird to then sit for ages and scroll through social media. This was helpful as it meant I engaged with the people I wanted to engage with but didn't end up going down internet rabbit holes or getting dragged into comment threads that don't make me feel great.*"

—VERITY CRAFT, General Manager & Storyteller, Intelligent Ink

17

Install a Newsfeed Blocker
LEVEL 1

A feed blocker on platforms such as Facebook, Instagram and YouTube removes all the distractions from your news feed and lets you focus on what you want to do—like responding to comments, posting updates, or replying to messages. If you wonder what a particular person is up to, you can always check out their profile. Blocking the feed reduces the noise and can make you build more meaningful relationships with the content you consume.

There are plenty of plugins for laptop browsers as well as smartphone apps that do this for you. Simply search online for "news feed blocker" or "news feed eradicator" and your device name. If you just want to scroll for a bit, simply turn off the blocker temporarily. Just make sure to turn it back on!

A short note on the word "feed": have you ever considered what this means? One way of looking at a feed mechanism in technology is "something that provides new input when available". A physical example is an ammunition belt that feeds cartridges into a gun. The challenge with social media feeds and news feeds are that **there is always something new available.** And what happens when we get fed too much? We get full!

18

Create Buffers in Your Calendar
LEVEL 2

This practice is important for anyone working in an office but even more crucial when working remotely. Many people have back-to-back online meetings with 30 seconds in between if they are lucky. Make sure to build in at least 5 minutes (ideally longer) between each meeting. Use those 5 minutes to stretch or move away from the screen.

Tips for Success

Block out time in your calendar for breaks. If that requires letting other people know that you'll be unreachable for that time, make sure to let them know. You can also look into changing the standard meeting time from one hour to 45 or 50 minutes—the quality will improve, too! More and more platforms, e.g. Google Calendar, are responding to this with versions of "short meetings".

19

Start a Fake Commute When Working Remotely
LEVEL 2

Commuting has its downsides, but it does create a clear distinction between work and home. If you are working from home a lot, try the fake commute. It is as simple as getting dressed and going out for a 10-minute walk in which you mentally prepare for work. Some people even pack their work bag and bring it on the walk to further the feeling of transition!

Tip for Success

Doing this again at the end of the workday provides an opportunity for proper closure.

"A fake commute is essentially an optimized morning routine designed to create a distinction between home time and work time. It provides structure to days that otherwise feel like they all blend together."
—ASHIRA PROSSA, Forbes Magazine

20

Close Your Browser Tabs
LEVEL 2

Have you ever had so many browser tabs open that they become virtually too small to see? I sure have.

Tabs are like wild thought trains, and it is so easy to just open up another one, and another one. They can be useful, but we need to commit to closing them after we have made use of them. Having multiple tabs open makes it harder to find the page you need, and invites distraction. Not only that, but we may also get FOMO and a bad conscience from all the tabs we are not dealing with, leaving a bit of our attention and focus is trapped in them—a perfect example of attention residue.

So, close down those tabs. It will feel scary, but you can do it! Perhaps at the end of every workday, or whenever you have more than five open. And while you are at it, do it on your phone too! If this feels impossible, take some dedicated time to address/action each tab, and then close them. If it turns out you really needed the tab, you can easily find it again from your browser history.

Some of us use tabs as a kind of "to-do list". In that case I suggest to move the tasks (perhaps including URL) to an actual to do-list which gives much more overview and possibility to plan and execute.

"I have been known to keep browser tabs open for weeks—even months—before finally plowing through that New Yorker long read or adding those best albums of the year to my Amazon Music queue. But with the expectation of getting a new work laptop today, I decided to do a little browser maintenance over the weekend, and after 10 minutes of trying to deal with each tab before closing it out, I finally just said 'screw it' and closed them all . . . and I felt instantly free."

—JOEL CUNNINGHAM, journalist and
    deputy editor of online platform Lifehacker

21

Help Your Organization Balance Tech and Life

LEVEL 2

Defining clear digital boundaries, expectations, and habits for its workforce can lead to increased productivity in an organization and to a less stressed, more rested, and positive work culture.

Consider these questions as a start:

- What does digital wellbeing and tech-life balance mean for us?

- How do our staff members rate their current tech-life balance?

- What challenges do we experience around technology?

- How can we address these challenges?

- What expectations do we have on availability and responsiveness internally and externally?

- How can we ensure that staff disconnect properly from work obligations outside of work?

- Which channels do we use and for what? When do we call someone, when do we email, when do we send a chat message or text?

- Discuss the value of deep work. How can we create a culture that protects an individual's productivity and focus balanced with team collaboration?
- What technology is okay to use during meetings?

"Lead by example, highlighting the importance of disconnecting, regularly checking in about their holiday plans and making sure this gets scheduled/blocked in the calendar early on and then planning around this—as well as having regular conversations about workloads, to ensure they disconnect not just during the holidays but also regularly in between."

— Karin Reiter, Global Head of ESG/Sustainability at The Adecco Group

II

TECH-LIFE BALANCE & MENTAL HEALTH

ADDICTION AND TECHNOLOGY

THE TERMS "SMARTPHONE ADDICTION" AND "social media addiction" are thrown around a lot, but it can actually be quite difficult to determine whether something is a habit or an addiction.

Consider this: **a habit** could be scrolling through the news or social media on your phone for 15 minutes while you drink your morning coffee. You do it most days, but it is not the end of the world if you miss it, and you have no issue stopping.

An addiction, on the other hand, might be if you regularly have a hard time stopping after those 15 minutes. You end up being late for work or fail to do important tasks, come into conflict with people about your device use, or feel distressed if you are unable to do your morning scroll.

While *technology addiction* or *internet addiction* is not clinically considered an addiction, *Internet addiction disorder (IAD)* is listed as a disorder by the American Psychological Association, and *Gaming disorder* is acknowledged by the World Health Organization. If you suspect that you or someone close to you might be suffering from Internet addiction disorder, the best thing to do is to contact your healthcare provider. It is important to understand that unhealthy technology use can be related to underlying issues. There are therapists, counselors, and coaches who specialize in both changing technology habits, and identifying and dealing with any root causes.

> *"As a result of mindfulness practice, I could see the anxiety coming from my Instagram addiction. It became abundantly clear that my job as a social media influencer and content creator was 100% damaging my mental health."*
>
> —GEORGIE ST CLAIR, former influencer turned digital wellness coach and mindfulness teacher.

Social Media

Few technologies have been so debated—so loved and hated—as social media.

Many also consider it the number one reason why smartphones are so addictive. While the term social media implies that it makes us more social, it has also been found to increase our feelings of loneliness. But it all depends on how we use it. If we spend hours every day using social media as a substitute for human connection, our feelings of loneliness are likely to worsen. However, if we use social media to deepen existing relationships or create new, meaningful connections it can improve our sense of belonging. We can use it to communicate with family and friends around the world or seek and offer emotional support.

"When the Internet is used as a way station on the route to enhancing existing relationships and forging new social connections, it is a useful tool for reducing loneliness. But when social technologies are used to escape the social world and withdraw from the "social pain" of interaction, feelings of loneliness are increased."

—THE UNIVERSITY OF MANCHESTER AND THE UNIVERSITY OF CHICAGO, 2017.

However, it is *also* easy to end up in a loop, going in and out of social media but having a hard time putting it away fully.

The Self-Perpetuating Loop of AGT

Unbalanced use of anything can create a cycle that is both negative and hard to escape.

1. If we feel e.g., stressed, lonely, or anxious, we use social media because it feels good in the moment, relieves boredom, and might make us feel more connected to others.

2. By using social media in these situations, we suppress the negative emotions and fail to address them. Our fear of missing out can also increase, along with new negative emotions and feelings of dissatisfaction, isolation, and inadequacy.

3. These new feelings increase our initial emotions of stress, loneliness, or anxiety.

4. To relieve ourselves of these worsening emotions, we seek a quick way out and use social media more, starting a new cycle.

Information Overflow

By the 1900s, human knowledge had doubled approximately every century. But by 1945, it was doubling at a rate of every 25 years, and with the current development of the "internet of things", some have claimed that it will soon double every 12 hours! Possibly an exaggeration, but it speaks to the vast availability and collection of information in our modern age—which brings with it several complexities that affect our wellbeing and can bring uncertainty to people's lives.

Access to information is a blessing and a curse. The speed with which knowledge and information now evolves and changes means that what we learn today may soon be redundant or wrong; the jobs that students prepare themselves for may not yet have been invented; and fake news makes people distrust politicians. We are presented with an excess of choices and alternatives, which makes making "the right choice" close to impossible. And not only is the volume of worldwide accumulated knowledge exponentially growing, so is the flow of it into our daily lives.

> *"Mass production has given us easy access to very large stocks of information. Finding information is no longer the problem, but being discriminating, filtering it out, and managing it is difficult. Quantity rises, but quality and balance drop. The long-term impact of these changes on the health of people and societies has yet to be seen, but many believe it will be negative unless we find a way to manage the flow of information into our minds and around our organizations."*
> —ANDREW WHITWORTH FROM INFORMATION OBESITY.

Digital technology has facilitated our access to, and intake of, news from around the world, 24/7. From previously knowing only what was happening in our little village, our radius of news has grown to include our region and our country, until today when we at any given moment can read about what is happening anywhere in the world. Immediate updates about world events have become the norm, a little-scrutinized part of everyday life. But there is growing evidence that consumption of news can cause increased anxiety, depression, and stress. Sometimes the news matters to us, other times it does not; but most of the time, we are consuming negative information without a chance to do anything about it.

So much of the information that we take in is neither connected to us, nor relevant to our decision-making process. We make the mistake of thinking that we need to form an opinion about everything, and in doing so we waste time and energy on fruitless endeavors. In today's world, it is also hard to avoid being exposed to information; it's common to find large screens in many public spaces, endlessly bombarding us with eye-catching content.

The Fear of Missing Out (FOMO)

It is a human drive not to miss out on things. During certain times in our history, not missing out was even vital to our survival. With the abundance of information that we have now, anxiety at the thought of missed opportunities has become a serious issue. This fear can drive us to return to social media, news platforms, or even our email inbox over and over to make sure that we respond immediately to someone's comment or post, that we don't miss an invitation to something, or that we are not left out of a conversation at work or with friends. All the while, FOMO is reducing our wellbeing and negatively impacting our mood and life satisfaction.

Sleep

Ever been scrolling your feed in bed only to realize it's suddenly 2am? It's old news that electronics disturb our sleep, but AGT has introduced a whole new set of challenges. Apart from causing us to lose track of time and go to bed later, devices also disturb our melatonin production, resulting in less sleep of lower quality. Melatonin is a natural hormone released by the body in the evening to help us feel tired and ready for sleep. Unfortunately, the blue light that most of our devices emit reduces and delays the production of melatonin in the evening, which in turn decreases the feeling of sleepiness and increases our alertness. The light can also change our sleep cycles and reduce the amount of time we spend in Rapid-Eye Movement (REM), where dreaming occurs, and in deep sleep.

Contrary to what some believe, passively scrolling through social media is *not* relaxing. It might feel good in the moment thanks to that pre-programmed dopamine release, but it winds our brain up and makes us excited and wanting more rather than making us relaxed.

> *"Checking your phone stimulates the brain so we are more active and awake, even just a quick check can engage your brain and delay sleep."*
> —SLEEP DISORDERS SPECIALIST,
>   Harneet Walia, MD

Decision-Making

Imagine that you go to the store to buy toothpaste. Upon arriving at the hygiene section, you note that there are seemingly *hundreds* of toothpaste types. You pull out your phone to check options online and find even more. There's strong, mild, peppermint, strawberry, whitening, with baking soda, with hydrogen peroxide, gel, with plastic-free packaging, 100% natural, activated charcoal, gum restoring, for cavity prevention, for tartar control . . . and the list goes on.

If you are anything like me, you will stand there with your mouth open and no idea which one to pick. How do I make the best decision? There are simply too many choices! With more choices available, we are more likely to feel like we've made a mistake, and more likely to get stuck in feelings of regret. Research suggests that **maximizers**, i.e., people who always try to make the best decision, tend to be more depressed and have lower life satisfaction than **satisfiers**, i.e., those who accept a good enough solution and move on.

With technological advances, we live in an era of nearly endless choice. No other generation has had this many choices, and the Internet and social media have both served to visualize all these different options. This applies to everything from everyday consumption to bigger life choices: dating apps like Tinder have enabled people to have hundreds of options of whom to date at their fingertips; we can buy clothes from anywhere in the world; we can spend hours comparing prices on that seemingly simple purchase; and we can browse jobs available all over the world.

The result? We are paralyzed by indecision, less satisfied with what we have, and second guess the choices we have made. And this increased number of alternatives is supposed to be helping us?

. . . . .

We've now had a look at some of the many ways in which AGT is affecting mental health. You probably recognize yourself in some of the references, and other perspectives may be new. Think about your own situation as we will now move in to how we can improve mental health in relation to technology use!

22

Use Social Media Intentionally
LEVEL 1

I would not have written this book if it was not for social media. It's true; a long chain of events led to me and my publisher, Andrew Flach, starting a discussion on technology over social media and email, which subsequently led to this book. Social media can give us a lot, but we need to be absolutely clear with ourselves on how and why we want to use it.

One way is to make a simple social media strategy, something that defines and limits your application of the technology:

1. This is what I want to get out of social media:

2. This is how I will get what I want:

3. This is where and when I want to use social media:

4. This is how much time I want to spend on social media:

If you're struggling to answer #2, a suggestion could be "less passive/mindless scrolling and more direct messages to friends/family or consuming content of specific interest." But any action that leads towards your #1 will support your tech-life balance.

23

Reflect on Your Social Media Use and Information Intake

LEVEL 1

Answer these questions as honestly as you can. There is no right or wrong.

1. Which social media platforms are you using?

2. What do you do on each platform?

3. How much time do you spend on each platform?

4. How do you feel when you think about social media?

5. How do you feel after you have used social media?

6. Which are the benefits of your social media use?

7. What are the negative sides of your social media use?

If you don't use social media, reflect on how much information you are consuming in a day. Do you feel overwhelmed by input or are you striking a balance? Do you walk around with music or a podcast playing constantly? Do you read the news on the bus? Answer emails or scroll social media during lunch?

"I really think social media is the most addictive thing in our phone. If you take it out of a phone it is a camera, maybe a bit of WhatsApp, a map and music. If phones only did that, our screen time would be completely different numbers. Those things aren't so addictive to our brain. Our brain is addicted to what other humans are doing, we are so conditioned to observe one another's experience and see how we can adapt ours. It's what humans have always done."

—TJ POWER, Mind Consultant

24

Reduce the Number of Social Media Platforms
LEVEL 1

Have you ever made an active decision about which social media platforms to use? Or do you typically just download new apps as they come out?

For this practice, determine which platforms you *want* to use by considering these questions:

1. Do I get enjoyment out of it?

2. Do I spend more time on it than I want?

3. Do I use it for my own benefit or for other people's expectations? How do I feel when I go off the platform?

4. Does it enable me to build meaningful relationships?

5. Does it make me stressed?

6. Does it serve any other purpose that is important to me?

7. What would happen if I stopped using it?

For those platforms that do not pass the 'test' above —get rid of them! Or at the very least, delete the apps on your phone. You can always keep the accounts if you change your mind in the future.

The choice of which platforms to keep will be up to individual need and preference. But if you do want a recommendation for a place to start . . . apps for picture and video sharing are often considered the most addictive

> *"I used to spend a lot of time on Facebook talking to people and scrolling through the newsfeed. I had all these excuses for why I couldn't delete it, like missing out on events, or losing touch with people. But when I finally got over those and did delete it, the excuses turned out to be false. I still heard about the events I wanted to go to, and still stayed in touch with the important people. It just blocked out all the noise."*
>
> —HECTOR HUGHES, co-founder
> of Unplugged.

25

Schedule Social Media-Free Time

LEVEL 2

Determine for yourself a time or place that is social media-free. This can be done in plenty of ways, but here are some examples:

- Weekends.

- At work or at school.

- Mornings before a certain time / evenings after a certain time.

- Bus/train rides.

- Bathroom visits (!)

Tips for Success

Determine what works for you. If you're planning to unplug during a time when you have traditionally been active on social media, try to let people know in advance—especially if they are used to getting replies quickly. Combine this with the practice of minimizing notifications! While you're at it, why not use the phone to remind you?

"For the first weekend, I went totally cold turkey and didn't use social media at all. The second weekend I allowed myself to reply to conversations on social media platforms and to use social media after the kids had gone to bed. My conclusion was that I was so much happier during and after the first weekend as I hadn't been interrupted or felt the urge of checking social media. I realized how much time I spend on social media and that it makes me less present in situations and conversations with others. I also realized how much others around me are utilizing their phones, and how bad this looks/ feels when being together. So this was definitely an eye-opener for me and led to me taking actions to balance my use of technological devices."

— MICHAELA, Sweden, who tried out social media free weekends.

26

Limit your Social Media Time

LEVEL 3

Determine how much time you want to spend on social media, and stick to your limit! If you need help, there are actually functions on most smartphones to set app limits to support you. You can of course do this with any other type of apps that you feel take up more time than you want.

Odds are that this will also make social media more enjoyable. As you remove some of those dopamine spikes, your brain will adapt to the new levels and make social media into something special instead of something you do to fill time.

Tips for Success

Replace all that freed-up time with something else that you like to make it enjoyable rather than just restrictive. For more, see the practice of finding healthy dopamine substitutions on page 91.

27

Enjoy *Without* Sharing
LEVEL 2

The next time you experience something and get the urge to share it on social media, think about *why* you are sharing it. Is it to share an experience with loved ones? Or, as it is for many people, is it subconsciously about getting that external recognition for the cool things you are doing and to get kicks from the likes?

The next time the feeling strikes you, try not to take a photo or video at all. Instead, try to be fully present and enjoy the moment instead of worrying about capturing it. Or else, take a photo for yourself to look at later, or to send to a specific person with your thoughts on the experience.

> *"Relative to taking pictures for oneself (e.g., to preserve one's memories), taking pictures with the intention to share them with others (e.g., to post on social media) reduces enjoyment of experiences. This effect occurs because taking photos with the intention to share increases self-presentational concern during the experience, which can reduce enjoyment directly, as well as indirectly by lowering engagement with the experience."*
>
> —Journal of Consumer Research

28

Delete Apps on Your Smartphone
LEVEL 1

Marie Kondo, author and organizing guru, says, "Every single item in your home should either have a purpose or spark joy." She has changed many people's lives by helping them declutter their homes and—really—our digital 'home', the smartphone, should be no different.

Go through each app on your smartphone. Do you use it? If not, the choice is easy—delete it!

Does it have a purpose or spark joy? If yes, keep it! If not, get it out of there!

Next, do the same on your laptop with any software you have installed.

Write down the apps you deleted in your notebook!

I cannot help you decide if an app sparks joy, but to support your decision on whether or not something has a purpose, try checking the stats on your phone to see when you last used the app. Don't be nervous—you can always reinstall it in a while if you desperately miss it!

Did you know?

The average smartphone user has 80+ apps but only uses nine of them daily and 30 of them monthly.

29

Remove Those Cute Background Photos

LEVEL 2

Sounds harsh, I know. I used to have a cool case for my phone, a cute picture of one son as a lock screen image and my other son as background.

But then I realized that every time I picked up my phone, I also triggered an emotional moment and warm fuzzy feelings. It felt absurd when I realized I was hard-wiring myself to associate my phone—a tool—with my love for my children.

For this practice, remove pictures of kids, partners, cute dogs or cats from backgrounds and lock screens on the phone. Maybe even your laptop, too, if that's a source of attachment.

Still feel like you're missing it? Why not go old school and print a photo to keep in your wallet? Or better yet . . .

30

Get a Supportive Lock Screen
LEVEL 1

If you want to go a step beyond just removing your cute background and lock screen, you can replace it with a message that supports your journey towards intentional technology use.

You can find a few suggestions to download for free at www.tainobendz.com/lockscreens.

31

Reclaim Your Sleep
LEVEL 2

Picture this. It's 9pm and you are watching a Netflix show, and suddenly...it's midnight. Or it's 10pm and you are just going to check your phone before sleeping and before long you've scrolled away two hours.

AGT is keeping us up later at night than we intend and it's negatively affecting our sleep quality. But there is also a part of modern culture—one which AGTs plug into—that glorifies working late nights and only getting a few hours of sleep per night. We have gotten so used to controlling our surroundings and getting what we want when we want it, but sleep is one thing that we cannot control and that is also vital for our wellbeing.

Reflection Exercise

Think about your current sleep habits and whether you are happy with them or not. Do you have a hard time falling asleep? Do you wake up in the middle of the night with your mind racing? Are you tired or alert when morning comes? Is your use of devices affecting your sleep?

32

Device-Free Bedroom
LEVEL 2

This is such a simple trick, but it's one that can have a huge effect. In one 2018 study, participants shared that leaving their smartphones out of the bedroom improved their sleep, reduced anxiety, improved their relationships, and prevented them from wasting time.

What about a tablet purely used for bedtime reading, you ask? It's up to you to determine if having that present winds you up or relaxes you. However, keep other tablets, TVs, and smartphones out of there!

> *"Every night, I would take my phone to bed with me, and be on it until my eyes were literally closing. I've even dropped it on my face a few times from falling asleep! I thought trying a phone free bedroom would be hard, but it really wasn't; there were even benefits that I didn't expect. It really helped reduce my anxiety by making a space in our house that I didn't feel overwhelmed in. This then meant I slept better, got back into reading books, and was present with my partner and kids."*
>
> —ZOE, New Zealand, who tried out phone free bedroom

Zoe's tips for success:

- Start by just having a phone free bedroom every second night, or just do it on weeknights, and then slowly move to every night.

- Allow yourself to check your phone as soon as you get up. I charge mine overnight and then enjoy checking it before breakfast.

- Keep post-its and a pen by your bed, so if you do think of anything you must do on your phone, write it down to do in the morning.

- Find a book you really like so you have something to look forward to doing when you go to bed. This way, you don't feel like you're missing out not having your phone to entertain you.

33

Get an Alarm Clock

Simple as that. Just do it—whether it's a $5 one or a $200 one does not matter, as long as it's a physical clock to help you regulate your sleep schedule. And no trying for one of those alarm apps on your phone—that's the slippery slope we are trying to avoid at bedtime!

34

Turn Off Your Phone Fully
LEVEL 1

When was the last time you consciously turned your phone off? Not to silent, not to sleep, but *off*? For most people, the answer is, "I can't remember!". This is a simple trick to show your phone (and your brain) who is in charge and build up your own sense of control.

So just turn it off.

Right now.

How does it feel?

Having devices always on or on standby/sleep makes resuming use simple, but it allows stress and tasks to carry over from day to day because we never get full closure, nor a fresh start.

Take a minute to bring your device-use to a closure each day. Close down your tabs, save work in progress, quit any open applications, and power off the device.

> *"What is the difference between being absorbed in a book and my smartphone? A book also has a pulling force and gives dopamine hits, but when I close the book I don't crash. Getting the dopamine from reading requires effort."*
>
> —ANNA TEBELIUS BODIN, author, speaker, and expert on the learning brain

35

Device-Free Curfew

LEVEL 2

There is a wealth of benefits to be had from discontinuing screen use just 30 minutes before bed.

While smartphones are typically the most common device to use before bedtime, tablets and the TV affect us too. Simply turn off the TV, put away the laptop, tablet, and phone 30 minutes before your normal bedtime. If you live with other people, do this together and engage in some non-tech activity together. You can also set yourself up for success by scheduling night mode/bedtime mode on your devices and even setting an alarm on the phone 30 minutes before your bedtime saying, "Put devices away, time for bed!"

If you want to take it one step further, try establishing a relaxing bedtime routine with activities that promote sleep rather than those that excite you.

"The challenge has been interesting for me. Normally I would be reading news, checking Instagram and searching the internet for information. Results: I have read three books and am loving the time and space that has been created to make this possible. I hadn't read a book for at least 6 months. I am definitely not as consumed with checking the news all the time and I am thinking about deleting Instagram as I am far more conscious about my screen time. These changes are now permanent, and I am certainly enjoying the less screen time and the change in my routines."

—MARY, New Zealand, who tried being
    device free 30 minutes before bedtime

36

Device-Free Morning
LEVEL 2

Imagine waking up in bed and immediately having your boss, your colleagues, a couple of friends, a news anchor, and a celebrity start talking to you, filling your brain with input before you've barely woken up. How would you feel? How would your day start?

This is exactly what we are doing when we check our phone first thing in the morning.

Whatever our mood is in the morning, it stays pretty much the same throughout the day. If we start stressed or in a bad mood, we typically end the day grumpy. If we instead start the day in a happy or calm mood, we are more likely to stay that way and be more productive too.

So let your devices stay unused for the first 15 minutes in the morning and re-claim your day! Choose carefully how you spend those first minutes in the morning and decide on a few activities that make you feel good or supports you, e.g., planning your day, showering, making coffee, eating breakfast, meditating, exercising, reading a book, or even calling a friend.

"Normally I would check my emails first thing, still in bed. I thought that it would make me get one step ahead, but it was also stressing me. I would also fall into mindlessly checking social media updates. During the two weeks of trying this challenge, I instead took time the night before to prepare for the next day. I still used my phone as an alarm but did not pick it up further in the morning. It felt like a much healthier way and gives me a calm and pleasant morning. I forgot a few times the first couple of days and started scrolling, but now I always remember and wake up actively thinking 'I will enjoy my morning and not check the phone.' I give this practice 9/10!"

—YASMINE, Sweden, who tried out device-free morning

37

Reduce Your News Intake
LEVEL 1

Limiting the amount of news you consume on a daily basis is a great way of reducing the digital noise in your life and can have quite a big impact. Start by identifying why and how you are currently consuming news and consider these questions:

- What is driving your urge to check the news?
- Which and how many channels are you using?
- How much time are you spending on it?
- How do you feel?
- Does it make you understand the world better?
- Does it help you make better decisions?

Balancing staying up-to-date with not getting over-whelmed can be tricky, especially if you are used to consuming a lot of news. Find a level of news intake that works for you.

Some will revert to the evening TV news, others will focus on local news, others still may need to limit themselves to a 30-minute check-in once a day with a news app.

"I was really surprised that I had so many apps on my phone regarding news. I don't need so many. I was able to limit the news I accessed, and I have not felt that I was missing out."

— MADELEINE, New Zealand, who tried out reducing news intake

38

Perform a Digital Detox

LEVEL 2

Getting a clean break from our devices can support building long-term healthy habits for everyday life. You might feel anxious initially, but you are likely to feel less stress once you realize that you can actually do it.

A digital detox can be done in many different ways. If the idea of going away for a weekend without devices is daunting, do a mini version at home. For example, try a phone free day, or a social media free day. Better still, build natural digital pauses into your daily routine: schedule breaks from your phone, go offline at 8pm each night, and have device-free zones or times.

"My life hack is I do not use any electronic devices one day a week. We chose Saturday because it really feels like the weekend day, and Sunday's the day when people start to kind of ask questions about things that are going to happen on Monday.

"So, on Friday night, my wife and I take our devices, we take our children's devices, and we lock them up. And we spend Saturday like a family in the 1990s or '80s or '70s, a time before screens. And we are bored sometimes, and we play board games, and we go for hikes. And we sit around, we talk, our kids complain about being bored, and it's great because kids don't get the opportunity to be bored anymore.

"So that's something that we've been doing for about a year and it has vastly and dramatically improved my life."

—Guy Raz, NPR contributor, podcaster, and author of the book *How I Built This*

39

Create Boundaries Between Work and Leisure
LEVEL 3

Technology has made it so easy to keep working in our leisure time, like writing an email at the playground or looking over a document while cooking. While it might feel impossible for people in high-paced jobs to create boundaries between work and leisure, these delineations are essential for long-term well-being. Doing so will reduce the risk of burnout and actually improve your productivity, not the other way around. And here's another cool thing—by giving your brain a pause and letting your subconscious process all the information you have taken in, you are also quite likely to get new ideas and come up with solutions that you did not see before.

Start by determining your core working hours. This will be different for everyone, and many people need some flexibility, but far too often fluid working hours result in more hours worked and less work done!

Cut down on "just checking" your work phone and "just a quick look" at your emails in evenings and

weekends. Maybe even put the work phone away? Whatever it takes to convince your brain to disconnect from "work mode."

Establish clear communication procedures. Make it known that you will typically not check emails after work hours but that you are available for calls (or not) if there is an emergency.

Tip for Success

Combine this hack with the practice of making use of the automatic reply!

40

Reflect on Your Internal Triggers

LEVEL 3

Do you ever end up in a perpetual loop with social media, browsing news, playing games, or looking at videos?

Don't just zone out during times like these. Instead, try to pay attention to what you feel like when you are using technology unintentionally. Reflect on what feelings or events trigger these actions.

Here are two examples from my own life:

Unwanted habit: Scrolling LinkedIn mindlessly or clicking around news sites.

Trigger: Feeling down or unmotivated.

Unwanted habit: Opening a new tab browser tab, switching tasks, and losing focus.

Trigger: Stress from not progressing fast enough or not getting new ideas and thoughts.

Once you have identified these triggering behaviors or feelings, it is time to find new replacement habits.

Find Healthy Dopamine Substitutions
LEVEL 2

Finding activities or actions that replace those short-term feel-good bursts that digital tech provides can have a huge impact on our long-term well-being and entire way of living. It also makes changing habits much more enjoyable. First, think of activities that make you feel good. These include activities where you think "I am glad that I did that" when you are done. Write them down in your pad. It should be activities that are easy to fit in during the day.

When the triggering emotions come up and you feel the need for a dopamine kick from your phone (e.g., when you are nervous, stressed, bored), instead do one of the activities you have identified. Reflect on how you feel.

Here is what it looks like for me:

Unwanted habit: Picking up the phone and scrolling social media mindlessly.

Trigger: Feeling down or unmotivated.

Replacement habit: Taking a five-minute breather, doing a few push-ups, or talking to someone.

Tips for Success

Here are some common activities to manage our mood in healthy ways:

- Do a quick exercise like 5 squats or push-ups.
- Go for a walk (even better with someone!).
- Meditate or just take 10 deep breaths.
- Eat a piece of dark chocolate.
- Read a good book.
- Play with an animal.
- Talk to colleagues, friends or family face-to-face or on a video call.

To support your transition, it can be worthwhile to introduce hindrances to give yourself time to reconsider when the urge comes. Several practices in this book are great barriers making mindless behavior harder. For example, moving apps away from the home screen; deleting apps on the phone; changing your phone's lock screen to remind you. This practice requires hard work and *can* be uncomfortable. If you think that you or someone else has serious underlying issues, you may want to contact your healthcare provider.

Control Your Wearables

Wearables can be great, but they are also an additional source of potential stress, and an aspect of technology that many people forget about. Using wearables also means that our bodies are constantly connected. Does it benefit you? Think about how you can get what you want out of your device—and nothing else—instead of going with the device's defaults.

Perhaps you use a smartwatch, but have you considered turning off Bluetooth during certain times of the day? Or stop wearing it at night? Managing the notifications? Have you considered *why* are you using it?

> *"My stress from being constantly connected had been building up for quite some time without me noticing it at first. I was also not conscious of how related it was to my smartwatch, despite working in the IT industry! It got to the point where I was about to collapse, and one morning decided 'I am done with you' and literally took off my smartwatch and threw it off of me. It gave an immediate impact where I felt calmer and more focused straight away. I have not put it back on since, and you know what? I have not missed a single important message, call or event."*

—KRISTIAN, Sweden

43

Five Minutes Alone With Your Thoughts
LEVEL 2

Pick a time of the day that works best for this, ideally a spot that you would normally fill with technology. Set a timer for 5 minutes and do . . . *nothing*. Don't consume any information around you. Stare out of a window at nature or close your eyes. This is not meditation; you can let your mind run freely!

> *"The more uncomfortable this exercise is for you, the greater the need. The brain is designed to think, not consume. If you can gradually increase to 10 minutes of being alone with your thoughts per day and do this for a month, a brain scan would show a visual difference in the brain's synapses. You will have physically strengthened your brain's network on impulse control."*
>
> —ANNA TEBELIUS BODIN, author, motivational speaker, and expert on the learning brain.

If you struggle, start with two minutes, but either way try to keep it up for a few weeks. How does it feel? Did it get easier? You might be surprised by the results!

"I did 5 minutes of nothing each day for two weeks as part of my morning routine. I was initially really hesitant to start the habit as I always feel like I have so much work to do. Once I started, I realized that taking 5 mins out didn't affect my productivity and probably even helped it. Initially, it felt really awkward but by the end of the first week, it was my favorite part of the day."

— GEMMA, New Zealand, who tried out
    five minutes with her thoughts per day

44

Meditate Regularly

LEVEL 2

The constant connectivity and high stress that many people experience on a daily basis can both make us breathe more shallowly and leave our minds constantly racing. It is a two-way relationship—one where anxiety affects our ability to breathe and where the way we breathe also influences our anxiety levels.

Start by becoming aware of when you feel stress building up, or when you notice that your breathing is shallow. Meditation can then be as easy as taking a few deep, conscious, breaths in through the nose and slowly out through the mouth. You don't even have to call it meditation if that does not feel like you. If you do sit down for a few minutes, just try to focus on the sensation of your breathing. When thoughts pop up, notice them and bring your attention back to your breath.

Tip for Success

Are you finding your mind wandering, or aren't sure *how* to focus? There are plenty of guided meditations online and apps to support you!

Staying Screen-Free After Work
LEVEL 3

Those of us who use a laptop or computer as the main working tool, rack up 6-10 hours of screen time each day from work alone. Keeping your after work hours screen-free can therefore be a great way of giving your brain and eyes a rest, not to mention improving relationships at home and leaving space for personal development. You will be surprised how much time there is after work when we ditch the devices! This is of course the same for those of us who don't use a screen as the main working tool.

If you struggle to go fully screen-free, set a time limit that works for you and is in line with your vision of how you want evenings at home to look. Replace the time you used to spend on devices after work with something that you enjoy or would like to do more of.

And if you feel like you simply *cannot* do this for your work, raise the discussion with your workplace. What expectations do we have on availability? Can we agree to call if urgent so we do not need to check in on emails? Or set up an auto-reply!

46

Make Use of the Automatic Email Reply

LEVEL 1

The automatic reply is a great way of managing response expectations and taking pressure away from constantly checking your emails. Many of you already use it on weekends or holidays, but why not use it every day? Simply turn it on when your core working hours end. For best efficiency, let people know how to get a hold of you in an emergency and when you will reply to their email.

This is the message that I turn on every day at 5pm: *"Thank you for your email. I typically check my emails at 9am and 2pm. If your message cannot wait until tomorrow, please call me at [phone number]."*

For social media, why not update your status to "Enjoying life offline" or a nice cover image stating that you are not online? Try it and see if it can change how often you feel the need to check in.

47

Evaluate the Well-Being Impact of Your Digital Activities
LEVEL 2

Below are questions connected to common activities that many people do every week using their digital technology. Paradoxically, we typically spend more time on activities that have a negative impact on our wellbeing than the ones with a positive impact. Why? The ones with a long-term positive impact give us a much slower dopamine release compared with the quick reward feeling of other activities!

Go through the list and closely consider each question, and the activity's impact on your wellbeing. Once you are done, brainstorm ways to spend more time on the activities that you want more of and that promote your wellbeing, rather than those offering nothing more than that quick dopamine hit!

- Do I enjoy reading e-books? If yes, do I actually read or do other activities come in the way?

- Do I use the phone while on the toilet? Am I happy that I am doing it?

- How do I feel when I check my phone for notifications? Do I ever feel controlled by it?

- How do I feel when I passively scroll social media? How do I feel after?

- Do I use health or wellbeing tools? Do I want to use them more?

- How does looking at content before sleep affect me? Is it hard to fall asleep?

- Do I use the phone in the car? How does it affect my driving?

- How do I communicate with others? How do the different channels affect my wellbeing? E.g. making a video call, texting/messaging, commenting/posting on social media. Which of these activities actually develop meaningful relationships?

- Do I dual-screen (e.g. use the phone while watching TV)? Why? How does it affect my enjoyment of the activity on each screen?

- Do I use devices during face-to-face conversations with others? Why? How does it affect my interaction? Do others do it to me?

- How is reading/sending emails on the phone after work hours affecting my stress levels and family life?

- Do I play games on devices? Am I happy with the way I spend that time?

- Do I use a learning app or site regularly? Would I like to? What would I like to learn?

- How and when do I listen to music/podcasts? Do I actively listen or just have it on? How often do I not have any sound input at all?

- How much news do I consume? What do I get out of it? How does it affect my wellbeing?

- How much time do I spend watching videos? Am I happy with the time spent? How do I feel after?

"Our findings strongly suggest that limiting social media use to approximately 30 minutes per day may lead to significant improvement in wellbeing."

—UNIVERSITY OF PENNSYLVANIA

48

Switch from Phone to Laptop

LEVEL 2

Did you know that most apps that you use on your phone can also be used on a laptop?

Obviously email and web browsing can be done anywhere, but apps like WhatsApp, Instagram, TikTok and Facebook all have desktop versions that can be browsed on your computer.

What's the difference? Desktop versions are less addictive as they are less accessible, meaning it's easier to be more purposeful by checking in a few times per day. (It's also much easier to type on a keyboard, but maybe that's just me!).

Decide which apps you definitely need on your phone, i.e., those you need to have access to all the time. Just remember: that means the apps have access to you, too. For the rest, switch to using them on the laptop on your terms.

Tips for Success

Let people know how to contact you for more immediate responses if they are used to you being constantly plugged into social media.

49

Single-Screening
LEVEL 2

Using two monitors for your laptop can increase your productivity but switching between your laptop screen and your phone will do the exact opposite. Just like using your phone while watching TV diminishes the experience of both and can increase stress. If a device does not deserve your full attention—turn it off! Single-screening is about being intentional with your device use and taking control of your time and device experience.

Think about which devices you tend to use simultaneously and focus on one device at a time.

Here are a few combinations to consider:

- When using a laptop, put the phone away.

- When using the phone, don't have the TV on too.

- When using the TV, put the phone and laptop away.

> *"I hadn't really noticed how often I do a quick message check or similar when in a work meeting and by not doing more than one thing at a time I was getting more out of the time I put into tasks and meetings."*
>
> —ERIN, Australia, who tried out this hack

50

Stay Safe Online

LEVEL 2

Online safety is not a focus of this book but is massively important. Failure to stay properly protected in the online space can lead to your tech-life balance becoming seriously out of control with things like identity theft, phishing, and other types of frauds and scams. Here are a number of practices to consider, pick a few to try:

- Limit the personal information that you share.

- Keep privacy settings on.

- Browse safely, don't click on dubious content online or in emails.

- Don't share sensitive information on public networks ("open WIFIs").

- Consider using a VPN.

- Be careful what you download; use trusted sites.

- Choose strong passwords.

- Use different passwords for different sites.

- Change password on a regular basis.

- Make online purchases from secure sites.

- Be careful what you post.

- Be careful who you meet online.

- Keep your antivirus up to date.

- Always update software to latest version.

- Delete old online accounts no longer in use.

- Always update software to latest version,

- Be aware and learn to spot fake emails and websites

- Cover your webcam (e.g. with sticky tape)

If you want to know more about this, there are plenty of free resources online for both adults and children/teenagers. For families, see more on page 147 on teaching kids to stay safe.

Unfortunately, as technology advances, so do the ways of using it to exploit others. We can only guess what the online/digital environment will look like just in a few years' time, but safety, being cautious and thinking twice will remain key factors in staying safe in the digital world.

51

Turn Off Auto-Play
LEVEL 1

Auto-playing videos and songs on streaming sites removes the conscious choice of engaging in a digital experience and is a big culprit of unintentional binge-watching. While it might feel counterintuitive to turn off a function that is there to make watching easy, this introduces some well-needed friction and forces you to make a conscious decision to continue after every video or episode.

> *"I would sit down to watch an episode of my favorite show, which then became two, three, four episodes as it just kept playing. I had never considered turning that function off but when I tried this for two weeks, I felt like I got my evenings back! I also enjoyed the show more as it became more special. I'm keeping auto-play turned off for sure!"*
>
> — ELLA, United States, who tried out turning off auto-play

52

Try a "Dumbphone"
LEVEL 3

When we buy a smartphone, we get plenty of functions that we want and need, but also so, *so* many that we don't . . . yet we end up spending a lot of time and attention on them anyway.

Dumb phones are not as dumb as they sound. A better name might be simply "mobile phone". These are devices without all the functionality that brings on detrimental effects and sucks in our attention. There are simple versions mainly used for texting and calling, and other more advanced versions that include some smartphone functionalities but without all the bells and whistles.

Determine which functionalities that you want, then go online and get yourself a less distracting phone!

"For a long time, I had felt that my balance between enjoying using the phone, and destructive scrolling was off. I used to wake up happy, but after a 2-minute scroll I was overloaded. I wanted to get rid of my smartphone but still wanted some functions like maps and podcasts. I keep my old smartphone in a drawer and take it out to use it purely as a tool e.g. for banking. Switching to a 'dumbphone' has only been positive."

—OLLE, Sweden, who tried a dumbphone

53

Limit Your Communication Channels

LEVEL 1

With the rise of smartphones and apps, the number of communication channels that we use has massively increased. As with many other aspects of AGT this might sound like a good thing—more is better, right? But when we think about it, the multitude of channels can also increase stress both in terms of receiving notifications, but also with the feeling of being on top of everything. Count how many channels you are using and see if you can limit your use to only the ones that are necessary or add the most value. Doing so will better allow you to take control over how people can demand your time and attention.

> *"It feels crazy when you add them up but I use 14 different channels. Voice calls, text messages, WhatsApp, Viber, WeChat, work email on Outlook, private email on Gmail, Skype, Teams, Slack, Zoom, Tik Tok, Facebook, Instagram. As a part of this experiment, I decided to focus my attention only on five of these that I enjoy the most and work email which I need. It has made a huge difference and I feel less stressed and scattered"*
>
> —JACK, United States, who tried reducing the number of digital communication channels

54

Tech-Life Balance During Holidays
LEVEL 3

The plan will look different for everyone, but the key is to take control and make A Plan. This can ideally be done together with the family or other people you spend the holidays with for maximum buy-in. This is not intended to be a detailed schedule to stick to, but a guideline to lean on.

Consider questions like:

- When we go back to work/school and look back on the holidays, what do we want to be able to say that we spent a lot of time doing?

- What do you need right now to relax and recharge? How will we make these activities happen?

- Which devices should we bring and what do we want to use devices for during this holiday? How much do we feel is reasonable to use devices for these activities? How can we use screens together, to bond and have family time, rather than isolating ourselves one by one?

- How do we feel about social media? What do we want to use it for and what is our fear of missing out founded on?

Have fun with it! Maybe try a version of a "swear jar" so that every time someone picks up the phone outside the plan they have to pay up.

This can be done in an organization as well:

Discuss with your team/colleagues how often you will check emails, what authority they have to make decisions, and when they need to call you. This clarity will let you relax and empower them as leaders and employees.

Some of us need to be available and check in with work over the holidays, perhaps even daily. Instead of doing it on the phone 10x a day, try scheduling a time in the morning and the afternoon when you read and respond to emails on the laptop.

55

Take Control of FOMO
(Fear Of Missing Out)

LEVEL 3

Have you heard of JOMO? The Joy Of Missing Out?

This is a mindset where you are happy and content with the choices you make and focus on what you *are getting* instead of what you are *missing*. If we accept that there will inevitably be things we miss, perhaps we can even find joy in not trying to know everything and being everywhere. To make things easier, especially related to social media, you can ask your friends and family to invite you to events through text messages, so you can relax knowing that you won't miss the important things in your life but can let go of the noise. To kickstart your journey towards less FOMO, try taking a break from social media. It's tough at first but can work wonders if we find joy in our life instead of the lives of others or our online life.

> *"The Joy of Missing Out, or JOMO, is FOMO's cooler cousin. When it sees that party of a friend of a friend, it doesn't jump at the opportunity. Instead, it politely declines and revels in not being there. JOMO doesn't decline every social opportunity, but it knows when to say yes and when to say no".*
> —DANIEL RILEY, Medium Magazine

56

Learn to Love a "Good Enough" Decision
LEVEL 3

With the endless possibilities tech offers, making the right decision is close to impossible—and as such, brings along a lot of stress. Whether you are choosing what to wear for the day, which words to use in that email, what to have for dinner or which laptop to buy, go in with the mentality of making a "good enough" decision. Not the perfect one, not the best of all possible options; instead, identify a few key choice criteria and pick the first option that meets them all.

If you can learn to love a good enough decision, instead of constantly searching for the perfect one, odds are you will feel much better and have less decision regret!

> *"Whenever you need a new laptop, call up one of your maximizer friends and say, 'What laptop did you buy?' And you buy that laptop. Is it going to be the perfect laptop for you? Probably not. Is it going to be a good enough laptop for you? Absolutely. It takes you five minutes to make a decision instead of five weeks and it's a 'good enough' decision."*
> —BARRY SCHWARTZ, psychologist and author of The Paradox of Choice

III

TECH-LIFE BALANCE FOR PHYSICAL HEALTH

ONE OF THE MOST EASILY NOTICEABLE AND quantifiable negative effects of improper tech use is its impact on your physical health.

Heart

By nature, sitting with a digital device reduces our physical movement which has several health implications. In a study published in 2021, researchers with the American Heart Association (AHA) found that adults under the age of 60 who spend a large part of their day sitting during leisure time are at a much higher risk for both heart disease and stroke.

Neck and Back

Sitting down also leads to back and neck problems, an issue that has become increasingly common with handheld devices, resulting in the new disease "Tech Neck". With the rise of laptop use, we sit with bent necks even when we are not on the phone. Our heads weigh around 10–12 pounds (ca. 5 kg), but as we bend our necks, the pressure on the spine increases with the angle. This can also happen when reading a book, of course, but we typically adjust our postures or stop reading when becoming uncomfortable—whereas with AGT, we might not even notice!

Poor posture can also cause muscle strain, pinched nerves, herniated discs and, over time, can remove the neck's natural curve. Apart from neck issues, it can reduce lung capacity by as much as 30 percent and it has even been linked to headaches and neurological issues, depression, and heart disease.

Hands

Handheld devices also affect the hands. A hand specialist I see because of a basketball injury says that he started seeing patients around 2015 for hand issues related to technology use, and since then it has only increased. "Trigger thumb" or "Texting/scrolling thumb" is a tendon inflammation caused by doing the same movement over and over again, e.g. when scrolling, texting, or gaming. I pointed out that I had seen a person in a brace in the waiting room sitting and scrolling. Consider that again: a patient with his hand in a *brace,* waiting to see a hand specialist, reflexively continuing to do movements that are harmful to his hand.

Eyes

Staring at screens for a prolonged time affects our eyes, too. Computer vision or "digital eye strain" is experienced by around 70 percent of American adults and can cause symptoms such as dry and tired eyes, headaches, and blurred vision. People who spend two or more continuous hours at a computer or using a digital screen device every day are at the greatest risk for developing computer vision.

Ears

With endless music streaming through increasingly efficient headphones playing close to our eardrums, tech related hearing loss is becoming an increasingly common issue. Our ears can get affected both by the loudness of the noise, as well as the length of exposure. A pair of headphones at max volume sits right between a lawnmower and a rock concert in terms of loudness and can damage our hearing in minutes.

Obesity

Have you ever watched TV with a bowl of potato chips next to you? If you are anything like me, all of a sudden, the bowl will magically be empty. To me, it is no surprise whatsoever that research supports the notion that we don't think about how much we eat if we are distracted:

> *"Eating in the presence of distractors increased the total calorie intake by 15% with higher lipid ingestion. These results showed that smartphone use during meals, as well as reading a printed text, significantly affects the number of calories ingested."*
>
> —LUIGI VANVITELLI, University of Campania

This of course does not mean that you cannot enjoy a meal in front of the TV every now and then, but for many people, consuming content from a screen while eating is an everyday occurrence, which may not be ideal.

. . . . .

There are plenty of other indirect implications too, with everything from accidents caused by using devices while driving or crossing a road and chargers electrocuting people in the bath, to injuries caused by dangerous selfies. Try some of the following practices to support your physical health!

57

Take Walking Meetings
LEVEL 2

This is one of my favorite hacks and I apply it both work and private meetings. It is also one that surprises many people with the real difference it makes. Apart from the obvious wellbeing effects of a walk, other benefits include improved creativity, memory, productivity, and collaboration.

For work meetings, let the other participants know that you feel like you need to move and get some fresh air. If you are meeting in person, suggest that you go for a walk during your meeting.

If you are meeting online, inform them that you are going for a walk and will have the video off. Plug in your headphones, mute when you are not speaking, and enjoy the walk!

If you are catching up with family and friends, simply suggest that you go for a walk instead of a coffee, or else combine the two. A walk is a much more memorable experience than sitting down. Remember to keep your devices tucked away and focus on each other.

"I work at an insurance company and spend most of my day sitting down with lots of online meetings whether working from home or in the office. I took one walking meeting per day for two weeks and absolutely loved it. I felt less tired at the end of the day, less stressed, and I got more done after the walk. Oh, and I couldn't multitask during the meeting! Remains to see if I can keep up the good habit!"

—SARAH, United States, who tried out walking meetings

58

Reflect on Your Situation
LEVEL 1

Have you experienced any negative physical effects from using technology? Common effects include neck pain/ stiffness, lower back pain/stiffness, elbow pain, thumb pain, tired or dry eyes.

Note them down separately, along with how often you typically get them.

Revisit your notes after incorporating some of the practices and see if anything has changed!

If you need tips on making positive movement changes, check out hack #61.

> *"Eventually, those subjects who managed to stick with the (movement) plan experienced an overall decrease in stress and a 15% increase in productivity."*
>
> —FROM RESEARCH BY DR. JAMES LEVINE

59

Use the 20/20/20 Rule

LEVEL 1

Many people get caught up in the screens and forget to look away, or even to blink, which can easily lead to eye strain. This practice provides anyone working on a digital screen the opportunity to reduce the risk of eye strain by simply looking away from the screen regularly.

Look away from the screen every 20 minutes at an object that is about 20 feet away for a full 20 seconds. Hard to remember? Set a timer and this micro pause can do wonders for your focus, too!

60

Take 15 Minutes Outside Per Day
LEVEL 1

It is easy getting stuck indoors, both at work and afterwards. This is especially true when you are just so tired that you fall down on the sofa and leave it to Netflix to give you your fix of "relaxation". However, it is on those particular days that you most need to get outside!

Being outside for just 2 hours per week has been shown to give a huge boost to both our physical and mental health. And better yet—it does not matter how those 120 minutes of nature time per week are achieved (e.g. one long vs. several shorter outings); what matters is taking yourself out of your normal environment and truly unplugging to appreciate nature, breathe fresh air and smell the roses.

This practice can be done in so many different ways and in any setting. Even in heavily urbanized areas, you can always find a tree where you can do some stretching or to read a book under. Why not use tech to help you? Set a timer on your phone at 9pm each evening for "Turn me off and go for a 15 minute walk"! (Getting a dog does it, too!)

Remember to Move It, Move It!
LEVEL 2

Workouts are good for our health, but what might be even more important is to move regularly during the day and not be sedentary for long periods. Leading an active physical lifestyle can reduce our risk of developing anxiety disorders by 60 percent, according to some research.

Here are some fun ideas to get you moving, moving:

- Put time in the calendar for 5-minute walks several times per day.

- Take walking meetings.

- Park far away from the office or get off the bus a stop early.

- Take the stairs.

- Go out for lunch or go for a lunch walk if working at home.

- Walk or stretch when you are on the phone.

- 5 squats every time you send an email.

- 5 pushups after every meeting.

- Stand up meetings.

62

Straighten Up
LEVEL 1

Even a slight tilt staring down at a smartphone or laptop screen increases the pressure on our necks significantly. Severe examples (which are all too common) of tilt can increase the weight load on the neck/spine by as much as 60 pounds!

To prevent this, keep your devices slightly below eye level instead of bending your back and neck. Get creative and use the things around you to prop up your devices!

63

Use the 60/60 Rule
for Headphones
LEVEL 3

Nowadays, we don't only listen to music or podcasts when we want to—we also put our earbuds in when we want to escape other noise. We listen more than ever (and often louder than ever) with high risks for hearing damage. Hearing loss due to the use of headphones is fully preventable if you don't use them too long or too loudly. Make sure your earbuds or headphones fit and work well, so you're not turning your music up too high

Consider the 60 percent/60-minute rule:

- Use headphones at **no more than 60%** of the maximum volume.

- Limit the amount of time you spend with head-phones to **60 minutes per day**.

60 minutes per day might feel impossible for many of us, so you can start gently by adjusting the volume. A good way to find out if your headphones are at a safe volume: ask people sitting near you if they can hear your music. If they can, it's a sign that your hearing may be getting damaged. Turn the volume down until other

people can't hear it. Keep in mind, too, that listening to music at a loud volume can make you unaware of what's going on around you which increases your risk of accidents.

Cultivating good listening habits today may mean that you can continue to enjoy good hearing in decades to come. Taking breaks after being exposed to noise can also give your ears a chance to rest.

And remember that just because a noise isn't annoying, it doesn't mean it might not be harmful over a long period of time.

> *"When volume levels exceed 85 decibels (dB), the hair cells of the inner ear can suffer damage. Your safe exposure time to sounds this loud (roughly equivalent to San Francisco street traffic) is eight hours. For every three-decibel increase in sound above that level, your safe listening time is cut in half."*
>
> —SAN FRANCISCO AUDIOLOGY

64

Let Driving Distract You from Your Phone
LEVEL 1

Even though we are 20 times more likely to crash while texting and driving than when not using a cell phone, around 40 percent of people still do it. Make a habit of always putting the phone out of sight in the car (unless using navigation apps). Pull over if you need to use it and use the Do Not Disturb While Driving function.

Stay safe on the roads!

"Texting is the most alarming distraction. Sending or reading a text takes your eyes off the road for 5 seconds. At 55 mph, that's like driving the length of an entire football field with your eyes closed. You cannot drive safely unless the task of driving has your full attention. Any non-driving activity you engage in is a potential distraction and increases your risk of crashing."

—US Department Of Transportation

65

Download a Wellbeing App

LEVEL 2

Do you want to start running? Eat healthier? Stick to a daily 10-minute workout? Start meditating? Think about what aspect of wellbeing that you want to work on and get support *from* technology by downloading an app.

IV

TECH-LIFE BALANCE FOR THE PLANET

OUR TECHNOLOGY USE HAS A BIG NEGATIVE impact on the world we live in. The most obvious are the consumption of resources needed to produce and run the devices and services, and the resulting waste. Just like other aspects of our way of living have a carbon footprint, we also have a digital footprint which is not nearly as well-known or considered. For example: did you know that over a year sending 20 emails per day can produce as much CO_2 as more than 620 miles (1,000) km of car travel? Or that, if the Internet was a country, it would be the third largest electricity user (after China and the U.S.)? Producing a computer requires around 50 pounds (22 kg) of chemical products, 500 pounds of fuel (240 kg) and 400 gallons of water (1.5 tons), and up to 90 percent of e-waste does not properly follow recycling routes! Other surprising stats include:

- With 4% of GHG emissions, digital technology pollutes more than the aviation industry.

- Online video streaming releases more CO_2 than the total annual amount of Spain.

- Bitcoin's electricity consumption exceeds that of whole countries such as Chile, Switzerland or New Zealand.

We upgrade to new devices with an increased frequency, as the producers make us feel like we absolutely need that latest model with the highest number of megapixels or a curved screen edge. There is a massive problem with e-waste, which often ends up in landfills in less developed parts of the world.

The other, and perhaps less obvious challenge that technology presents to our planet lies in our increased disconnection *from* the planet. As we spend more and more time in the online world, there is a real danger of our becoming alienated from not only people, but our planet, too. AGT takes our focus away from the world and nature around us. When the weight of the world becomes too intense, we flee into the digital world for a break and a quick feelgood fix; similarly, we can escape the degradation of the planet around us. An obsession with the technology in front of us, and perhaps the perception of ourselves in the digital world, has led to many people being more concerned with the "health" of the technology they use than the health of our planet.

> *"If we are to flourish in the information society then we have to think about how to make our relationship with information healthier and sustainable, and this is intimately connected to the need to create a more sustainable, healthy world."*
> —ANDREW WHITWORTH,
>   Information Obesity

As digital technology continues to evolve, considering how it affects our planet both directly and indirectly is more important than ever. Here are some principles to reduce your tech/planet impact and increase your connection with Mother Earth!

66

Re-use, Recycle!
LEVEL 3

Make sure to recycle any old devices lying around at home, especially when you are changing to a new device. There are plenty of organizations that safely recycle the material or that wipe all data, refurbish the device and sell it for re-use.

By the same token, if you're looking to upgrade your device and aren't committed to the absolute top-of-the-line model, there are plenty of near-new options available second-hand. Just search online for re-used devices. It's a great way to get new tech while consuming more sustainably. Before you choose to upgrade a device, however, take a moment to consider why you are doing it and if you really need to or if it can wait.

67

Consider Your Tech-Planet Impact
LEVEL 2

Think about all the ways that you use digital technology and the devices you have. How many new devices have you bought? How often do you change your devices? How much do you use services that require server space and thereby electricity, e.g. streaming services, email, social media? We might often only focus on the electricity use of our physical devices, and not on the data centers or servers enabling our use.

68

Embrace Self-Reflection

LEVEL 2

Instead of filling every dull moment with stimulation from technology, take the opportunity of those still minutes to reflect. What feelings come up? How do you feel about what is going on in the world? Do you feel attached to our planet? Can you change some of your consumption, both materialistic and of information, to connect with our planet and the people around you?

V

TECH-LIFE BALANCE FOR FAMILIES AND KIDS

DEVICES AND KIDS WERE THE MAIN REASON why I started deep-diving into technology habits and a large part of where I draw my passion from. All the challenges in the book are as relevant for children as for adults, if not more so. But the challenges children face are extremely different: their brains are still developing and are more plastic, and they still have a ton of skills to learn.

Just as for adults, it all depends on what, how much, and when we use devices. While devices can indeed be used to support child development, AGTs tend to fully absorb our young ones and pose some shocking risks. Children also typically lack the decision-making skills that adults have, meaning that they have a hard time making and executing the decision to pull away and put a device down.

In this section, I use the term "children" loosely to cover the whole range from babies, toddlers, preschoolers, up to adolescence. The context is very different depending on how old your child is, but across all ages parents are generally highly concerned.

Technology is directly related to the top three concerns that parents have, and indirectly connected to several of the others according to a 2020 U.S. national poll:

1. Overuse of social media

2. Bullying/cyberbullying

3. Internet safety

AGTs are also related to other concerns in the top 10, such as stress and lack of physical activity. And caregivers are right to be concerned!

The Impact of Tech on a Child's Development

Entire books have been written on this topic, and we will only touch on this briefly to acknowledge the risks. Our focus is on reflection to understand what is relevant for us and our children and how we can best support our young ones.

You might have seen alarming reports on screen time and kids' health and development. According to the American Academy of Child and Adolescent Psychiatry, unhealthy technology use can lead to sleep problems, lower grades, weight problems, poor self-image, mood problems, and more. You don't need to throw that smartphone out the window, shut down their TikTok account, or go cold turkey with their Roblox gaming. But I do believe that it is crucial to consider the effects and the alternatives, and to challenge the status quo.

Every age bracket has its challenges and unhealthy tech exposure affects them in different ways.

Under 5s

Just because an AGT makes them sit in one place or stop crying, it does not mean that it is the ideal problem solver or that it teaches them self-control. Some research-ers even argue that, by being distracted by AGTs, kids miss out on learning to control their frustrations and read emotions, and parents bypass vital opportunities at parent-child relationship development. These moments can both form strong bonds on both sides, and to ignore or skip them can lead to developmental delay.

AGT in this age group can also influence:

- Attention span and focus, as AGT provides stimuli but does not offer time to process input.

- Impulses and the ability to cope with frustration, as constant stimuli from AGT can make children forget how to rely on themselves for entertainment leading to frustration and the hindering of imagi-nation and motivation,

- A child's ability to read faces and learn social skills and thereby developing empathy.

"When I see children walking with a parent or being pushed in a stroller, they are often playing on a smartphone or a tablet and not paying attention to anything else around them. They will not learn about the world around them if all they're doing is looking at a smartphone. This will not just affect their ability to learn new things, but also how they interact with others and how language develops."

—Dr. Jennifer Cross, Attending Pediatrician and assistant professor at Weill Cornell Medical Center.

5 to 10-year-olds

Children at this age have mostly laid the foundation of social skills and learning so the challenges are slightly different. They can also use screens on their own in a different way: many own their own smartphone and often spend hours online daily. They typically have less supervision than younger children.

Typical challenges for this age bracket include peer pressure from friends to stay online, social comparison and coming across inappropriate content which can impact their wellbeing negatively, and a detrimental physical effect from passive device use.

Adolescents

In some aspects, teenagers might have the most challenges with AGT and are the hardest group to support in building healthy habits. Many of them grew up with this technology when it was still new and poorly understood and, for many, it is seamlessly intertwined with their lives. But this super-connected state comes with some steep costs.

One study found that almost 50 percent more girls and 25 percent more boys felt left out in 2015 compared to 2010. With constant connectivity and an increasingly large part of life being lived online, teenagers are seeing what everyone else is doing, which makes them aware of what they are missing out on. Loneliness and social isolation can cause deep distress. Other studies have shown a correlation between depression or anxiety and social media usage. But it is important to note that it can go both ways: one review from 2016 showed that the quality of social factors in the social media environment determines whether the effect on mental illness and wellbeing among adolescents is beneficial or detrimental.

Overuse of technology in this age group can also lead to lack of attention, lowered creativity, sleep disturbances, and negative effects on physical health. A study of teenagers aged 15–16 found that those engaging in digital media for longer times had an increased likelihood of developing symptoms of attention-deficit hyperactivity disorder (ADHD). Another study, from the National Institute for Health Research in the UK, of girls between the ages of 11 and 14 and identified a correlation between technology use and lower physical activity, higher BMI, and less sleep. The increased physical inactivity can also lead to chronic diseases such as diabetes.

Gaming and Addictive Behavior

Both gaming disorder and internet addiction present big challenges for parents. It can be hard to support a child through this; some parents even report children becoming physical when asked to stop playing a game or put down their phone. While some of the practices in this book will help you and your family balance the use of digital technology, including games, it is important to understand when to seek professional counselling, just like with any other problem that has gone too far for us to handle on your own or as a family.

Children's Sleep

Just like adults, device use before bed can increase the time needed for the child to fall asleep and cause them to feel tired the next day. According to one 2015 study, for example, infants 6 to 12 months old who were exposed to screens in the evening showed significantly shorter nighttime sleep than those who had no evening screen exposure. Another study found that kids who watched more than two hours of TV per day were 64 percent *less likely* to get the recommended 10 hours of sleep compared to those who were on a screen for less than 30 minutes per day.

· · · · ·

Learning about the impacts of AGT on children might leave you feeling depressed and hopeless. But there are plenty of things that can be done to support families and young people to build healthy technology habits!

69

Reflect on Your Family's Situation

LEVEL 1

As a parent, I know how busy life can be and how easy it is to just keep going. I invite you to take a moment to consider these questions about tech use and kids. Write your answers down in your notepad if you want:

- What positive experiences have you had with children and devices?

- What negative experiences have you had?

- Has your child expressed any concern about their technology use?

- Do you have any concerns about your child's technology use?

Considering these questions will hopefully give you a good determination to take on some of the other practices in this book. And even if you don't, it will have given you an increased feeling of control and consciousness.

Come back to your reflections on the questions above or your notes after incorporating some of these practices in this section and see if anything has changed!

70

Be a Role Model
LEVEL 2

Kids do what we do, not what we say. It's the oldest saying in the parenting book . . . and also so, so true. Many parents I talk to are concerned about their children's device use but at the same time they are checking emails at the dinner table or scrolling social media as soon as they think the kids are not noticing (or even when the kids *are* noticing!).

My first advice to parents is always this: Think about how you can model healthy and conscious tech use and showcase habits that you want your child to learn. Put away your phone when you come home and avoid using it when you are with the kids. Turn off TVs and other screens when not in use. Don't leave screens on in the background. Set clear boundaries between work and leisure (check hack #39).

Many parents I talk to struggle to stop working when they come home. They keep checking in on emails, being available on the phone, or even working when caring for a sick child. This was not possible just a few years ago but has almost become a norm. Talk to your boss and colleagues. Taking care of a sick child *and* trying to work is a sure recipe for stress *and* an upset child. I've tried it.

71

Measure Family Device Use
LEVEL 1

Having a proper understanding of how we use devices as a family or group lays a good foundation for change. Count how many devices you own (TV, tablets, phones, gaming consoles, etc.). Which devices do you use the most? How much do you use these devices (check device data or estimate)? Where at home do you typically use them? When?

This exercise is a great way to make the whole family aware of just how big of a part screens play in your life.

You can write the answers down in your notebook along with an estimation of how many hours each person spends on devices while at home.

> "I showed some of my lockable phone cases to a school class and this boy asked if he could bring one home. When I asked why, he said that 'My mum really needs one of those. She spends more time on her phone than talking to me.' I got so shocked and realized that this little boy had been reflecting on his mum's screen use and the negative effects on their family."

> —STEPHANIE SPINDLER JONSSON,
>   CEO MyPauze

72

Have the Tech Talk
LEVEL 2

Whether you choose to tackle this as a family or one on one, help to make your kids feel like a part of the process by listening to them without judgment, letting them understand why there are rules and why it is important, and collaborating in setting the rules at home. Try not to frame it as a punishment but rather as something important for the whole family to adhere to.

Some questions to discuss:

- What do we like about our devices? What do we dislike?

- Do we feel like devices are disturbing sleep, school/work, or time with friends and family?

- How much time do we want to spend on our devices?

- How do we feel after we have used a device for a certain activity?

- How would we like to use the devices differently?

- How can we make family time as fun as possible, so we don't even need devices?

Tips for Success

A good way of introducing the conversation could be to say that you have thought about your own device use at home and how you feel distracted, or that you have noticed that there are many conflicts around it. You can also make the conversation more enjoyable by having a nice meal with it! For more advice, check out the guides from the Center for Humane Technology available online.

If you have never had a family meeting before, there are also good resources available for free online.

"The number one thing that we can do to most effectively parent our kids and teens in the digital age is all about how we talk to them about screen time. The key around rules is getting their collaboration when possible, making sure they understand why there are rules, then adjusting them as needed, and checking in over time."

—Dr. Delaney Ruston, family physician, and creator of the award-winning film Screenagers

73

Help Kids Stay Safe Online
LEVEL 1

Just as we teach kids how to stay safe in the analog world, we need to educate them about the digital world, too. I encourage any caregiver to spend some time familiarizing themselves with this topic and reading more from credible sources online such as Common Sense Media, Center for Humane Tech, or government sites.

Here are a few starting points for online safety for kids:

Share with care. Limit sharing of images and personal information. Teach children to only share information with people they know, and help them understand that things that are shared online can stay there forever and end up in the wrong hands.

Be kind. Be kind online and treat digital communication like face-to-face communication; if it isn't right to say, it isn't right to post. Be aware of online bullying.

Be critical for fakes. Help kids become aware that online situations are not always as they seem by learning to analyze information critically and discerning between what's real and what's fake.

Online security. Teach kids to safeguard valuable information online just as they would offline. Talk about what sensitive information they know of such as passwords, personal information, any financial information, etc.

Talk it out. Acknowledge that just like in the analog world, the majority of people and content is good, but some are bad. Be open with the fact that they may come across something or someone inappropriate, and that they should never feel ashamed of talking to a trusted adult about anything they've seen or experienced that has made them feel bad.

74

Make a Family Device Plan
LEVEL 3

As we've noted several times, achieving **tech-life balance is more about being intentional than purely restrictive**. A good way of being conscious of our tech use as a family is to make a clear plan. Just like with everything else, children need rules that they understand and make sense for them to follow.

Making your own device plan can be as easy as agreeing on times when kids can use the devices and what they can choose to do on them. Plan it together with the child to create clear boundaries and expectations on when, how long, and what they will be used for. If you want to take it one step further or get more inspiration, an extensive planning tool can be found online from Common Sense Media.

The point is to make device use part of a scheduled routine. Many parents report that this has reduced conflicts and the need for any nagging.

75

Have Offline Areas and Times
LEVEL 2

Select a couple of places and times at home that are kept fully device-free/offline. This goes for the adults, too! Common choices for families are in the bedroom and during mealtimes, homework time, and family time.

> *"Keep bedtime, mealtime, and family time screen-free. Don't use screens in the car except for long trips, and consider setting a curfew or an agreed-upon time when your family shuts off all screens. Balancing online and offline time is extremely important."*

—DR. JENNIFER CROSS, child behavioral expert

Alongside this, keep usage of the TV as well as mobile devices like tablets and smartphones in the common areas of the house. This makes it less divisive and makes it easier to engage in their use and know what your kids are doing.

As a starter, why not keep meals device-free?

76

Do Fun Non-Tech Activities
LEVEL 1

Put family game nights in the calendar and experiment together with different kinds of games. Get a board game, or learn a new game with a deck of cards, or why not take it outside and kick a ball around or stage a treasure hunt? If you schedule weekly family time, an idea is to rotate and let a new person select the activity every week to keep everyone involved.

You can also help your child enjoy life *outside* of tech use by helping them get a hobby. There are hobbies that cost money, certainly, but there are plenty of free activities, too! With a little research and creativity, there is a lot to be found that your child will enjoy and that will support their development. Yes, it takes some effort, and yes, your child might be resistant at first, but you may find it really is worth it.

An abundance of ideas from creative low-tech parents are available a quick online search away!

77

Device-Free Meals

LEVEL 2

This practice might feel daunting to many. 'You mean we need to talk to each other again?!'

And yes, it might be a bit tough at first, like changing anything we have been getting used to. But I promise you, a good laugh and chat over dinner is way better for our wellbeing and relationships than a quick scroll. And if you live by yourself, mealtime is a great time for reflection rather than consuming stuff from devices. Research also suggests we get a better meal experience!

> *"Making sure that mealtimes are a technology-free zone is critical to family cohesion and means that every family member can be fully present whilst enjoying a nutritious and delicious shared meal."*
>
> —EMMA KENNY, psychologist and
>   behavioral expert.

Consider how you can make this a fun experience rather than only a restriction. Just remember that when you're putting the devices away, your pocket is not an acceptable place as it will still call on your attention!

It can be a bit awkward at first, and that is okay. Here are a few conversation topics if you need them!

- How did you help someone today?
- If you could have one dream come true, what would it be?
- If you could be an animal, what would you be and why?
- If you could meet a celebrity, who would it be and why?
- If you could decide your future, where would you be in 10 years?
- If you could have any pet, which and why?
- If you could trade places with your parents, what would you do differently?
- If you could trade places with kids, pick your own name?
- Which book or movie character describes you best?
- Which book or movie character would you like to be and why?
- What is your favorite vacation memory?
- What is something embarrassing that happened today?
- What is a challenge you overcame today and how?
- Name three good things that happened today...
- What is something surprising that happened today?

78

Follow Screen Time Guidelines
LEVEL 2

This is a great way of making device use with kids less about feelings and opinions and more about following official recommendations, just like we do with many other aspects of raising kids.

These recommendations are based on information from The American Academy of Child and Adolescent Psychiatry, the American Heart Association, the American Academy of Pediatrics, and the World Health Organization.

AGE	SCREEN-TIME & CONSIDERATIONS
0-18 months	None except for video chatting, i.e. actively interacting with others, along with a caregiver.
18-24 months	Very restricted, i.e. a few hours per week. Limited to watching educational high-quality programs with a caregiver. Engage with the child and explain what is happening on the screen.
2-5 years	1 hour per day for non-educational screen time. Focus on high quality and co-view to help the children understand what they are seeing and how to apply it to the world around them.

AGE	SCREEN-TIME & CONSIDERATIONS
6+ years	2 hours per day for non-educational screen time. Focus on high quality and engage in the activity. Discuss the experience with the child and make sure that you understand what they are doing and that devices are not interfering with sleep, physical activity, and interaction with friends and family.

Tips for Success

Discuss with other parents. If the parents of a group of kids that interact with each other follow roughly the same rules, it makes it a lot easier. Individual assessment is of course super important, as well as considering the *type* of screen-time and not only the time spent. For best buy-in—discuss together as a family! Try to make it a positive experience rather than a restriction. Engage in other activities with your child (see hack #76).

79

Follow Social Media Age Limits
LEVEL 2

Just like following official guidelines on the amount of screen time, following the age limits is not only good for your child but should make a strong argument at home.

These are the recommended age limits from some of the currently popular platforms themselves:

APP	AGE LIMIT
Snapchat	Over 13
WeChat	Over 13
TikTok	Over 13
Kik	Over 13
WhatsApp	Over 16
Facebook	Over 13
Twitter	Over 13
Instagram	Over 13

"I have seen questions from parents who have 8-year-old kids saying, 'I cannot get my kids off TikTok!' What they don't realize, is that an 8-year-old is really not supposed to be on TikTok in the first place. Like most social media platforms, it is a 13+ virtual space, although I would say that 16+ is actually a much more appropriate age limit."

—TEODORA PAVKOVIC, Psychologist and digital wellbeing expert

80

Delay Screen Time Introduction for Toddlers
LEVEL 2

This one is for those of you with children that have not yet been introduced to screens. Consider delaying the question of screen time limits and device rules altogether by holding off introducing your kids to screens until they're a little older. Some parents experience that having no screens at all is easier than budgeting and arguing. Even small children will get used to and will seek out the immediate gratification of a screen rather than enjoy the slow but more meaningful feedback of the analog world if they aren't given a chance to appreciate things in their proper context.

81

Avoid the Device Pacifier
LEVEL 3

The next time you need a few calm minutes or your child throws a tantrum, try to see it as a learning and bonding opportunity and *not* use the screen as a pacifier. Being there for a child when they are upset and co-regulating them to calm down is an important part of teaching them to handle their emotions in a healthy way and at the same time gives you an opportunity to show love and strengthen your bond. Teaching them self-control and to have fun with something else than a screen while you have to do something will benefit them in the long run!

My secret weapon is to have a special box with toys or games that *only* comes out when I need time to myself. Try it out—it works a charm!

Don't stress if you do use the device as a pacifier occasionally (I do!) but try not to make it a habit or it may become the only thing that can calm them down.

> *"A toddler learns a lot more from banging pans on the floor while you cook dinner than he does from watching a screen for the same amount of time, because every now and then the two of you look at each other."*

—Dr. David Hill, MD, Fellow in the American Academy of Pediatrics

82

Know That It's Okay to Say No
LEVEL 2

If your child is engaging in online activities that you deem harmful, or using devices in a way that you believe is having negative consequences in their life—it is okay to say 'no'! Using devices is not a fundamental right for a child, it is a privilege. And if you feel like you are being mean, remember that saying no can actually *help* the child better deal with their feelings.

Saying 'no' also becomes a lot easier after having gone through with practices like screen time talk (hack #72) and setting clear rules (hack #78). Here are a few other helpful tricks to use:

1. Give a short explanation. "We have scheduled your device use for later today" or "You need to finish your homework first".

2. Offer age-appropriate alternatives, e.g. "Why don't we read your favorite book?" or "Do you want to bring over a friend?" Be there for them to help them regulate their emotions.

3. Say no, but with an opening. "Great idea to play on the tablet. You cannot use it now, but we can play on it together after I have finished cooking"

4. Make sure you say 'yes' a lot when they come up with ideas and suggestions that are acceptable for you!

"Parents need to remember that they are allowed to say 'no' sometimes, but I often find that today's parents feel really uncomfortable doing that. Bringing children into the decision-making process is definitely a good idea in some cases, but other times it's fine to say, 'I am the parent and this is a non-negotiable in our family, and I don't need to explain it any further right now.'

— TEODORA PAVKOVIC, psychologist and digital wellbeing expert

83

Switch Passive to Active Screen Time

LEVEL 2

Shifting passive device use to active can relieve some of the detrimental physical effects and in some instances even improve our physical health. How would you compare 1 hour of playing a game like *Pokémon GO* outdoors with 30 minutes of watching YouTube videos? Or 1 hour of an online workout with 30 minutes of scrolling the news and social media?

The bottom line is that *not all screen-time is the same.* Find alternatives to sedentary, passive device use that the child enjoys, and switch some (or all!) of it to active use! You can of course do the same for yourself.

Suggestions for active alternatives:

- Interactive dance videos.

- Learning an instrument online.

- Learning a language online.

- Exercise videos or games.

- Games that involve physical movement.

"Emphasize the big three: sleep, healthy nutrition, and exercise. All three are essential to optimal brain growth and development and health and wellness for children and adults alike. And excessive screen time can impact all three."

—Dr. Jennifer Cross, child development expert

84

Choose Media Consciously

LEVEL 2

Do your research to find age-appropriate apps, games, and programs to let your children use. If your child wants to play a certain game or watch something, make sure to search online to find the age recommendation. You can also use information from organizations like Common Sense Media for reviews to guide you in making the best choices for your children.

85

Actively Decide When Kids Get a Personal Device
LEVEL 2

It is easy to fall for peer pressure or become convinced that the kids need their own device. Think it through properly before purchasing a personal device for your child. What is the reason behind getting them their own phone or tablet? What will they use it for? Why now? Do your research and have clear rules from the start on how much and for what they will be using it. If Bill Gates can do it, so can you!

> *"We don't have cellphones at the table when we are having a meal, we didn't give our kids cell phones until they were 14 and they complained other kids got them earlier."*
>
> —BILL GATES, founder of Microsoft

86

Engage in Kids' Device Use

LEVEL 1

Using tech together can have a positive impact on the relationship between caregiver and child, and also improve the technology experience for the child. Research and find age-appropriate activities that you can do together using a screen, or brainstorm together as a family. Choose together or let the child pick an activity.

Tips for Success

Combine with the practice of talking about tech (hack #72) so that the child feels involved and understands that it is not a punishment but a meant as a positive experience.

Suggestions for activities include:

- Watch a movie or show together with no other devices around.

- Online workout (Cosmic Kids yoga is great for younger children, and for the older ones, you can usually use the same as for adults).

- Play a digital game where the whole family can partake.

- Learn a new hobby together.

- Let your child find a recipe online and cook it.

- Make/play an online quiz.

"If children are going to have screen time, the best thing you can do is to watch the show or game with them to help them understand what they're seeing. Comment on things you notice, ask questions about what is happening, if someone on a show is singing a song, sing along with your child. Engage with them and repeat concepts after the show is over so they're more likely to retain that information."

—DR. JENNIFER CROSS, Child Behavioral Expert

87

Get Physical

LEVEL 2

Help your child to be physically active. Get them outdoor toys, go to a playground, engage in sports, or simply go out in nature for a game of hide and seek. Watch out—you might need to get active, too!

> *"Combining increased physical activity with reduced screen time showed a gradual beneficial effect on mental wellbeing across genders. One hour of physical activity and no more than two hours of screen time a day provided optimal mental wellbeing."*
>
> —DR. ASAD KHAN, Associate Professor, Researcher, University of Queensland

88

Talk To Other Parents and the School
LEVEL 2

If you are having conflicts with your children about screens at home, it is likely other parents are too. Talk to your school about what they are doing to support the kids in growing healthy technology habits and discuss with other parents what rules they have at home. If we can come together as a community with clear rules and expectations it becomes much easier for everyone, including the kids themselves. In fact, many schools around the world are starting to introduce technology policies at school. And just like with everything else, the more we can support our kids at home, the better the outcome outside the home.

We have collective agreements on rules and behaviors around other addictive objects that can be hard for kids to manage on their own. Why can't we do the same for technology? Answer: we can, but we need to put forward the effort to establish and stick to these agreements.

89

Keep Devices Out of Sight at Home

LEVEL 2

If you want the kids to eat less candy, would you leave sweets out on the kitchen table? We scan our environment constantly and often turn our attention to whatever is around us. So why not surround your family with things that you want to use more, and remove those you want to use less or differently?

Designate a place out of sight where you keep devices when they are not in use. This is great for adults, too, so put your phone in the same place and be a role model.

Tips for Success

- Combine with the practice of managing notifications (hack #1) and keep sound on for any notifications you want to be alerted of; e.g. calls
- Tablets and phones are obvious, but you could even cover up the TV with a nice piece of fabric.

We do this in our family, and I've noticed such a clear difference. When my phone is in sight, the kids will ask if they can play a game on it just because it's Right There. We have even covered up the TV and put away the remote, which means that they don't get as easily reminded that it is there.

> "Parents should cut down on their own screen time or explain what they're doing on their devices so kids aren't 'looking at the black back of the phone... [with] no idea what's going on".
> —SNAPCHAT CO-FOUNDER AND CEO EVAN SPIEGEL

90

Support Your Teenager

LEVEL 3

Raising teenagers can be a challenge in any aspect of parenting: they are semi-independent and old enough to make many decisions on their own, yet still very much under development and easily influenced. As a parent of a 4- and a 6-year-old, I have the highest respect for those of you with teenagers. Many of the practices in this section are applicable to teenagers, but might be harder to implement. I have talked to parents whose teenagers don't want to talk tech or simply ignore the agreed offline times and physically refuse to put down their devices.

This practice is more of an encouragement and a message. It is easy to feel overwhelmed and perhaps give up, but be aware that change can take time and that you are doing them a favor in the long run, just like with any other hard decision as a parent. Also remember that using digital technology is a privilege, not a right, and that you are (probably) the one paying for their device use and making it possible. Lastly, it might be helpful re-iterating that this is not about taking away their devices, it is about helping them balance screen use with other activities and teaching them to found a healthy relationship with these devices that they are likely to be using for the rest of their lives.

On page 217, you can read more about screens and teens from psychologist Teodora Pavkovic.

If your teenager uses the argument "well, everyone is doing it", they may very well be correct. And therefore, it might be helpful to talk to other parents and the school (hack #88).

VI

TECH-LIFE BALANCE FOR SOCIAL LIFE & RELATIONSHIPS

ONE OF THE MOST OBVIOUS EXAMPLES OF how AGT can have negative effects on our relationships is phubbing.

> **phubbing;** *the practice of ignoring one's companion or companions in order to pay attention to one's phone or other mobile devices.*
> —OXFORD DICTIONARY

Even if this is the first time you come across the word itself, odds are that you both have been a victim of phubbing and done it to others. While it might not seem like a big deal to check your phone while being with someone else, it makes you appear significantly less polite and attentive, can decrease relationship satisfaction in marriage, and even indirectly impact life satisfaction and depression.

Thinking back on situations where I have been phubbed (and yes, I have done it myself, too), this makes a lot of sense. When you are talking to someone who picks up the phone you may feel that you are not important, or even rejected and excluded. Then there's the interesting aspect that when being phubbed, we are more likely to reach for our own phones too, often to go on social media to battle those negative emotions of being ignored with a dopamine kick.

Another aspect of having constant access to AGTs through our smartphones is that we are more distracted, less able to enjoy in-person social interactions, and even experience reduced enjoyment of meals.

In fact, just having a cell phone nearby during personal conversations—even if no one is using it—can cause friction and trust issues.

Reflection

Have you ever phubbed someone? What triggered it? Have you ever been phubbed? How did it feel?

"When we use our phones while we are spending time with people we care about—apart from offending them—we enjoy the experience less than we would if we put our devices away."

—RYAN DWYER, University of British Columbia

Missing Out On Life

AGTs can distract us and make us miss out on what is important in our lives, regardless of whether it's something in our digital or analog life. Being absorbed by AGTs can make us miss out on the opportunity to use that technology with intent (e.g. I picked up my phone to start my meditation app but got stuck checking Instagram) just as we might miss out on something happening around us in analog life.

The problem is that we are not able to register what is happening around us when we are too absorbed by devices. In one study, 75 percent of college students who walked across a campus square while talking on their cell phones did not notice a clown riding a unicycle nearby.

> "Decades of research on happiness tell us that engaging positively with others is critical for our well-being. Modern technology may be wonderful, but it can easily sidetrack us and take away from the special moments we have with friends and family in person."
>
> —RYAN DWYER, University of
> British Columbia

A good term to describe this is **opportunity cost**. This is an economic term that basically means "the potential benefit we miss when choosing one alternative *over another*." Of course, with any decision we make we are inevitably missing out on something else, but AGT has a tendency of absorbing us so fully that we are not even aware of the time and attention we are giving up.

Typically, this occurs in those situations when you are "killing time" or afterwards feel like you "wasted time" on tech. When you spend longer than you intended on your devices, when you use the device mindlessly, or even without really choosing to, you inevitably give up on something you could have done instead. For example, when we scroll on the bus, the opportunity cost can be a calm moment staring out the window, or a conversation with a stranger; when we binge-watch Netflix, the opportunity cost might be talking to a friend, going for a walk, or reading a book.

> *"We can go to watch our kid play soccer, and we have our cell phone on one hip and our Blackberry on our other hip, and our laptop, presumably, on our laps. And even if they're all shut off, every minute that we're watching our kid mutilate a soccer game, we are also asking ourselves, 'Should I answer this cell phone call? Should I respond to this email? Should I draft this letter?' And even if the answer to the question is, 'No,' it's certainly going to make the experience of your kid's soccer game very different than it would've been."*
>
> — BARRY SCHWARTZ

Fake News and Filter Bubbles

Filter bubbles are a state of intellectual isolation that can occur when a site's algorithms select and recommends the content a user is most likely willing to see and engage in based on information it has collected about that user. For example, if I do a bunch of searches on Google about climate change being fake then go on to Facebook and share and engage in this type of content and go on YouTube and look at video after video being recommended to me . . . filter bubbles are likely to keep perpetuating one type of content in my feed without presenting alternative ideas, ultimately creating an ideological bubble.

Being intellectually isolated does not mean that I am alone in my bubble—quite the opposite, as strong groups can form in these bubbles—but the opinions of others, or even facts about other viewpoints do not even reach me. We are actively, or passively due to site algorithms out of our control, filtering out the information that does not suit us or support our worldview. It becomes a technology-enabled confirmation bias that can create a strong division.

Closely connected to filter bubbles is fake news. This phenomenon has been used throughout history for everything from swaying public opinion to entertainment, but digital technology has put fake news on steroids both in terms of the ability to spread news, and the difficulty of verifying every piece of information. Today, a deliberate lie can be spread to millions of people around the world in a matter of seconds. Adding to the problem is how many online business models encourage the production of "click-worthy" information or "click-baits". Just researching fake news has made me want to click on several dubious articles like the one about Hillary Clinton selling weapons to ISIS—789,000 engagements on Facebook, and verified fully fake.

While some fake news may be harmless, fake content relating to elections has had a huge spread and resultant impact. According to BBC, the top-performing false

2020 U.S. election stories had more millions more shares, reactions and comments on Facebook than the top real ones.

The inventor of the World Wide Web, Tim Berners-Lee, has even said that fake news is one of the three most disturbing Internet trends that must first be resolved if the Internet is to be capable of truly "serving humanity."

. . . . .

In this chapter we've noticed the interesting paradox of how technology can either aid or negatively impact our social life. The practices in the following pages are intended to help you reduce the detrimental effects and increase the positive impact of technology on your social life and relationships. We do it by changing how we use devices when we are with other people, as well as how we interact online.

91

Avoid Phubbing (Phone Snubbing)

LEVEL 2

In this practice, you are asked to be actively mindful of how you use your phone in the company of other people to avoid making them feel rejected and unimportant. While your phone can be an important part of modern life, human contact is a crucial contributor to health and wellbeing. By focusing on the person in front of you and not 'being somewhere else' mentally, you can improve the quality of communication, the relationship satisfaction, and even reduce your risk of depression.

> "This study tells us that, if you really need your phone, it's not going to kill you to use it. But there is a real and detectable benefit from putting your phone away when you're spending time with friends and family."
>
> —ELIZABETH DUNN, Professor of Psychology, University of British Columbia

Just like many of the practices, this can be hard at first—not picking up the phone when there's a lull in the conversation can feel forced or awkward.

Here are some helpful tips for success:

- Turn notifications off to reduce the distraction.

- If you really need to use the phone, let the other person know what you are doing.

- Leave your phone out of sight when you are with someone.

- Tell others how you feel if you are being phubbed.

- Unplug headphones when you are with other people.

92

Choose the Right Channel
LEVEL 1

The art of choosing the right communication channel is basically this: if you have something that needs immediate attention, call instead of sending a text or email. If we know through which channels urgent communication will come, whether work or private, it becomes easier to relax and not stress about constantly being on top of all our channels.

Both in your work and private life, consider the urgency of your message before sending it and choose a communication channel with suitable attention interference on the recipient's side.

Talk to friends and family and let them know how you want to communicate. Which channels do you want to use? If they need to get hold of you quickly, how do you prefer that they do it? Remember as well that your behavior sets their expectations on your responsiveness. If you want them to respect your wishes, you need to follow through on your practice.

You can also talk to your colleagues and leaders at work about improving the communication flurry. Do they also find it challenging and stressful? Work together to lay out some basic rules such as when to use the different channels and what responsiveness is expected on e.g. email, chat functions, calls. Which channels do we use with external stakeholders? See hack #21 for more tech/life balance options for organizations.

93

Reduce Your Number of Social Media Connections
LEVEL 2

This practice is the opposite of maximizing the number of followers and friends online. Go through your social media accounts and unfollow any people or accounts that you don't feel add positivity to your life, or that you do not feel connected with. Focus on quality contacts rather than quantity.

Perhaps you find some of these are people that you would like to deepen the connection with. In that case, see the next page and nurture that relationship!

Did you know?

In a famous study, Robin Dunbar, a British anthropologist, theorized that humans could have no more than about 150 meaningful relationships that we are cognitively able to manage and to which we can legitimately feel connected to at a given time. This is also known as Dunbar's number.

Take it one step further by also going through the contact list on your phone! Are you below Dunbar's 150?

"We're not designed to deal with thousands of people. We're designed to live in tribes of up to 150 people and have strong relationships in those tribes. When you're scrolling through social media, or checking messages, you're in communication with hundreds, if not thousands of people. We're just not wired for that. I think you've really got to approach that with care. Less is more."

—HECTOR HUGHES, co-founder of Unplugged

94

Nurture a Relationship Using Technology

LEVEL 1

There are good ways of using technology to improve relationships and reduce loneliness. Especially during times of physical isolation—such as during the COVID pandemic—this can be a really important practice and it is vastly different from scrolling social media.

Think of someone that you want to deepen your relationship with or that you have been meaning to talk to but haven't gotten around to. Engage with them in a personal way, be it with a call or a longer email or chat message. It means a lot more than liking someone's holiday pics.

95

Give Your Phone a Home
LEVEL 1

Select a place somewhere in your home, like a drawer or a box, where you can always keep your phone when not in use. Put it there as soon as you come home. This practice is perfect to stack with putting away your keys or wallet.

Tip for Success

Combine this with the practice of managing notifications so that you are only alerted for the things you want to be alerted of. Put the phone back when you have finished using it!

"At home, I left the phone on do not disturb and also left it in a bowl on the kitchen counter charging. Without the constant notifications I did not check it at all. This was amazing and allowed me to truly enjoy some time with my partner and time on a hobby."

—PHONE FREE DAY PARTICIPANT

96

Stop Messaging With Family During Your Day

LEVEL 2

Each time you message a family member, you are pulling away your attention from the present. You are go on mental stand-by while waiting to receive an answer, further scattering your focus.

While these might feel like meaningful interactions, many people report that the more they message during the day, the less conversations happen at home in the evening...leading to an increase in screentime to fill the void. Since we can get a much stronger connection when interacting face-to-face, it might be worth trying to cut out the constant messaging!

Does this mean you can never message your partner or family member while at work? Of course not! But I encourage you to try to reduce your back-and-forths to only when necessary.

> "One of the things I strongly recommend is for friends and couples to stop texting each other throughout the day. Instead, do a full catch-up/play-by-play at dinner, where you can engage and really listen to your partner."
>
> —Anya Pechko, Digital Wellness Coach and founder of Project Be

97

Get a Hobby
LEVEL 2

Think of something that you used to love doing but never have time for now (or perhaps something that you have always wanted to try that looks like fun) ... and do it together with someone! Why not put it in the calendar each week for a few weeks so that you really set yourself up for success? This is a great way to have some awesome non-tech time together that you will start anticipating! Maybe it's a new language, cooking, dance, playing an instrument, programming, design, or something entirely different like a magic trick. You can of course use technology for your new hobby too.

The internet is an amazing source of free knowledge that you would normally have to pay for anywhere else. So why not make use of it? This is also a great way of easing into using your devices differently. You are still using it for recreation, but you're engaged in creating a more sustainable and healthy dopamine release.

98

Fact Check and Deal with Fake Content
LEVEL 2

Fake content is getting more and more advanced and can reach you in the form of everything from a fake news article to fake emails to get your credit card details, to so-called deep fakes—videos where a person's face and voice have been replaced with the face and voice of someone else. Keep these points in mind when consuming content online:

1. **Reflect** on what you come across. Is it reasonable? Is it likely? Use a high dose of common sense and skepticism. If it seems weird, it probably is.

2. **Verify** unlikely content. Check the sources, and cross-reference against other channels if possible.

3. **Think twice before you click.** Is it just click-bait, an extreme headline meant to get you to click?

4. **Think twice before you share.** Read the entire piece and do some research before you decide whether or not to share. Don't become a part of the problem!

For verifying news specifically, check out The News Literacy Project online.

Another aspect to consider is so-called botting on social media. These are typically fake accounts with fake personalities and could make up as much as 10–20 percent of all accounts. These bots are partially or fully automated, often designed to mimic human users and frequently used with ill-intent, e.g. to increase the popularity of a person or movement; influence elections; manipulate financial markets; amplify phishing attacks; or spread spam. Social media bots continuously increase both in use and in mimicking skill and can be bought and sold on the black market. Apart from the points above, here are a few specific tips to determine if an account is a bot:

- Run a "reverse image search" on the profile picture to see if they are using a photo of someone else taken off the web.

- Look at the timing of their posts. If they regularly post at times of day that don't match up with their time zone or are making posts every few minutes every single day, this should be a warning sign.

- Use a bot detection service such as botcheck.me that uses machine learning to detect bot behavior.

If you come across fake content and want to do your bit, you can join the Digital Polarization Initiative or report fake news on Facebook.

99

Talk to Strangers
LEVEL 2

What does this have to do with tech? A lot! Whether we look down at our phone or walk around with our earbuds in, technology has made it so easy to look busy and avoid interactions with strangers. We forget that human connection is essential for our wellbeing!

So why not grab some of the opportunities that get presented to most of us during a day at the bus, in a queue, at the café, or in the elevator.

One study showed that participants who smiled, made eye contact, and chatted with the cashier when buying their coffee had improved moods after the interaction, compared with those who didn't interact beyond what was necessary. Other studies suggest that engaging with and trusting people we don't know is important for our wellbeing, the wellbeing of those we encounter, and even the health of society. Friendly behavior toward strangers has been linked to higher self-esteem in teenagers. In the United States and Canada, trust in strangers has also been correlated to individual wellbeing.

Talking to strangers might feel awkward at first, but I really encourage everyone to grab hold of these everyday opportunities. Who knows where they might lead you? Without exaggeration, during the last few years talking to strangers has directly and indirectly given me several job opportunities, new friendships, ideas for this book and much more. Most of us interact with strangers online more than ever, but when was the last time you did so in real life?

> *"Again and again, studies have shown that talking with strangers can make us happier, more connected to our communities, mentally sharper, healthier, less lonely, and more trustful and optimistic."*
> —From The Power of Strangers:
>   The Benefits of Connecting in a
>   Suspicious World by Joe Keohane

100

Observe and Reflect on Our Relationship with Tech

LEVEL 1

Start actively looking for people using AGT. What do you see? How are people around you using AGT? How are you using it? Is it indeed grabbing their attention? Can you spot anyone who looks like they are using it mindlessly? Do you feel like tech is used as a tool or not? Is it adding value? Do you see a lot of phubbing? What emotions do you experience?

Try to identify what opportunities that are missed by this way of using technology. Try to instill awareness in yourself of when you are "wasting time" and refocus your attention to spend this valuable resource on something or someone that makes you happy or supports your long-term wellbeing.

> *"Start observing your relationship with this tech because it is only going to be more and more. Now is the time to think—can I build a good strong relationship with it? A relationship where I find space away from it to just be a human being wandering around on this planet. I think that this relationship*

will be very powerful and significant for those who manage to build it in the decades to come."
—TJ POWER, Mind Consultant

AGT has completely changed the way we live in just 10–15 years, and odds are the rate of innovation will just continue to increase. New types of devices arrive, new technology gets developed, and the line between the digital and analog world gets increasingly blurred. Reflecting on our relationship with tech will be one of the key steps in ensuring that technology gives us more than it takes away.

I invite you to keep this practice as a mindset regardless of what opportunities and challenges future technologies may bring.

101

Get Lost and Live!

LEVEL 1

This final practice is about letting go. Stop trying to optimize every single part of your life using technology, stop obsessing over feeds and updates and emails and news stories and just...live life with its ups and downs, its mistakes and successes. As we've noted over and over again in this book, technology can provide great enhancements to our lives. But we are also increasingly using it to avoid the uncomfortable: the uncomfortable wait at the bus, the uncomfortable silence in a conversation, the hassle of reading a map, the awkwardness of asking a stranger or taking a wrong turn. But being uncomfortable or bored is an aspect of life that many claim is key to personal growth.

Confused where to start? Here is a very practical way of trying this practice: Try to find someplace you are going without using your phone's navigation. Select a restaurant by walking around looking in, or ask a stranger which is their favorite place, instead of checking online ratings. Walk over to a colleague and ask something instead of sending them an email.

Think about situations in your life when you use technology to "improve" and "optimize", and then think about how you can do it differently—not for greater efficiency, but for a richer experience of life.

> *"A couple traveling to Taipei wanted to go to the most famous temple but were not allowed to use Google maps as part of the study. They got lost on the way and stumbled across a hidden temple where they met the ward, sat down for an hour, and even got parting gifts. That is a unique experience they would have missed if they had followed the blue dot on Google Maps."*
>
> —Dr. Lena Waizenegger, Auckland University of Technology, referring to a study where the subjects were asked to travel without their phones

Who knows what unexpected events could unfold when you get lost and live?!

FINAL THOUGHTS AND LOOKING AHEAD

I T IS HARD TO PREDICT THE FUTURE. IT'S ESPE-
cially hard to foresee how technological advancements
will shape human life, and which innovations are yet
to come.

When I look at the technological evolution of AGTs
since the iPhone came out in 2007, and how it has
changed our lives dramatically so quickly, my thoughts
immediately go to the future. Not a hundred years from
now, but just a couple of years. A lot of mind-blowing
technology is already here with tech giants waiting for
the public to adopt (or accept?!) it, and for complemen-
tary technology to develop. With technology such as the
Metaverse, Neuralink, super advanced AI and machine
learning, digital assistants and self-driving cars, it feels
like we're living in a sci-fi movie at times.

But do we need all this? On an organizational level, we can have hardware and software robots working tirelessly 24/7, freeing up time for human workers to focus on value-adding tasks that require critical thinking. But there is also the risk of humans getting laid off as a result. On an individual level, there is already so much technology making our lives more efficient and freeing up time. With the rise of the internet of things, we may be able to free up even more time: the AI in the fridge senses that you are running out of juice and automatically places an order of your favorite brand, which arrives by drone to your doorstep. Your smartphone calculates the fastest route to a destination and your self-driving car takes you there. The smartwatch on your child lets you know the optimal bedtime that will shorten the time to fall asleep. The iPad babysits your toddler when you need a moment's rest.

Some would argue that with technological advancement, we can focus on more meaningful things in life. But what are those? What do we do with this freed-up time? And are not all of those moments that technology lets us bypass part of our human experience? Perhaps there is some value in making a wrong turn, running out of juice and going to the store, or mowing the grass instead of having a robot doing it. Maybe there is meaning in going out for a walk in the pouring rain instead of slipping on a pair or VR goggles and sitting at a beach in a digital world.

While I will not endeavor to discuss the purpose of life, I will bring up something top of mind for many of us: What is the secret to happiness? There is a suggested answer to this question from the Harvard Study of Adult Development, one of the longest-running studies on happiness. This study has followed over 700 men since they were teenagers in 1938. The participants came from various economic and social backgrounds, from Boston's poorest neighborhoods to Harvard undergrads. The men were contacted every two years with sets of detailed questions about their lives, as well as in-person interviews both with the subjects themselves and their partners, analyses of medical records and brain scans, and other investigations about their life, health, and happiness. During their lives, the participants in the study diverged into a highly varied number of careers, geographical locations, and family constellations. Some became rich, some poor, and one even became president of the United States.

From this spider web of different fates, the researchers could determine one common denominator for happiness:

> *"The clearest message we get from this 75-year study is this: Good relationships keep us happier and healthier. Period."*

> —ROBERT WALDINGER, Director of the Harvard Study of Adult Development

There are two nuances that we will note:

1. Social connections lead to happiness and health, and loneliness not only leads to less happy lives but also shorter ones.

2. The quality of the relationships matters more than the number. We want relationships where we feel protected, supported, and can count on the other person.

So, back to technology. With the knowledge from the Harvard study, is attention-grabbing technology making us less happy? I think so. Can we use the technology to become happier? I think so. But we need to be aware of what we are doing.

If we use the time that technology frees up to focus on relationships, I think that it can enhance our human experience and make us happier. Similarly, by being conscious we can use technology to create social connections with high quality. Rather than using technology and our time for growing our number of followers or friends base in the thousands online, we can use the same technology to connect closely and deeply with fewer people.

While many of the research studies that get published report on the negative effects of digital technology on our health, some claim that the worry is exaggerated and that it is too soon to draw firm conclusions about the impact of e.g. social media on mental health and also highlight the need for collaboration between researchers and technology companies.

The way I look at it, the research can be summarized in a fairly simple and logical way: if we spend excessive amounts of time using digital technology, we move our arms and fingers and sit in unnatural positions, which causes e.g. thumb, arm, and neck pain. We are also sedentary and less physically active, which increases the risk for a range of issues including obesity and heart diseases. We stare at bright screens close to us for long periods which affect our eyes and listen to music for extended periods with such good and loud sound that it damages our ears.

If we do things for the sake of getting positive feedback on social media and are too preoccupied with sharing our experiences online, it reduces the joy and memories of the experience, of our lives, and long-term wellbeing. If we go online to escape our feelings of loneliness or anxiety, our situation is unlikely to improve long term and we might instead feel worse.

If we take in large volumes of information close to bedtime, it affects our quality of sleep and time to sleep as our mind is wound up.

If we buy new devices too often it puts pressure on the earth's resources.

If we are constantly distracted, we cannot focus on our work, our studies, or the person in front of us.

But.

If we start again, using technology as a tool and not in an addictive manner—if we start using it in a balanced, conscious way—it can support our wellbeing, enhance relationships, make us more productive, and live a happier life.

With producer-driven innovation and an economy battling for our attention we need to start not only talking about tech-life balance, but making active choice; on how we use today's technology, how we best relate to the rapid innovation happening all around us, and what tomorrow's technology should be like. I hope that this book will continue to be relevant even some years from when I write this and when the technology has advanced from the kinds I am familiar with.

One thing that will remain relevant and never go out of time are those core questions: how do we healthily use technology without it taking away focus from our lives? How do I use technology consciously and for my benefit? How do I use technology with kindness and compassion? If I were able to instill one point from this book in you, it would be this consciousness to observe your own and others' technology use.

What the world needs right now is not more distraction. We need more connection to the people around us and our planet.

Thank you for reading my book and giving my ideas an honest chance. The knowledge, awareness and practices included in this book can without a doubt create value in your life and improve your health, focus and relationships. I would even go so far as to saying that they can change your life.

Just remember:

It is not what you know that counts, it is what you do with your knowledge that makes all the difference.

ACKNOWLEDGEMENTS

THERE ARE SO MANY PEOPLE THAT HAVE BEEN a part of making this book happen to whom I would like to acknowledge and express my gratitude. If you read this and are one of those amazing people who have supported me, cheered me on, challenged me, spread my work, participated in interviews shared quotes and thoughts for the book, and tried out these practices—a sincere thank you. You are a part of this book, and I very much recognize every one of you.

Without my first coach, John Maybury, I would not have started Phone Free Day—which subsequently led to a whole lot of exciting things, including this book. Thanks, fella! And thank you to all of you who have given your time to make Phone Free Day possible and help people around the world towards a healthier tech-life balance.

It´s been a pleasure to work with the team at Hatherleigh Press. Special mention to Ryan Kennedy, Ryan Tumambing, and Andrew Flach for believing in this idea in the first place, as well as the hard work of turning a chunk of text into the book it is now.

My curiosity for the world, interest to observe, and integrity to stand for what I believe in, all stems from my family—especially my mother and grandmother. I am happy that you raised me the way you did. And thanks to the greater family and all the in-laws for being part of the journey and supporting me in different ways.

Little Albert and William: you two give me so much and have made me look at the world differently. Your passion and enthusiasm for life is contagious and a big reason for me taking a stand for a more humane use of tech, for your future. Please never grow up; but if you do, keep that spark alive. I will do my best to fuel it.

Lastly, to my partner, Astrid. You always stand unfaltering by my side. Whether I want to publicly run a campaign about smartphone use, quit my job, write a book, or take up a yoga teacher training, your standard answer is, "Awesome! Of course you should do that!" That does not mean that you don't point me in the right direction when I am lost, come back with constructive criticism, or even stop me when I am chasing too far down the rabbit hole. Life with you is an adventure.

—Arohanui, lots of love.

Taino Bendz

FREQUENTLY
ASKED QUESTIONS

ONE THING THAT I LOVE ABOUT THE TOPIC of digital technology and our use of it is that everyone can relate. And generally, people are very keen on discussing it, and ask brilliant questions. While there is no right or wrong answers, I have collected some of the more universally relevant questions I have received and my thoughts on them.

Q: How do I strike the right digital balance while still maintaining strong human connections when in lockdown situations?

A: This is a spot-on question and very central in the whole topic of tech/life balance. It relates to being intentional and purposeful with our technology use. Social media scrolling can make a pandemic-driven isolation situation even more isolating, but a call (audio or video) to a loved one or a Zoom board game night can grow and maintain our human connections. For me, doing a live presentation online is a great example, which I feel maintains and deepens my human connections. The same goes for more personal one-on-one calls where both parties take the time to really listen and give the other person 100 percent of their focus (not scroll social media at the same time!). I have felt quite overwhelmed at times with chat messages from friends and family around the world, getting stressed out and then failing to reply...which I then feel even worse about! But a call, even just for 10 minutes, makes all the difference in the world.

Q: Yesterday I facilitated a Zoom meeting with over 200 participants. It went on for over an hour and a half and after that I was completely drained. Why does this happen and do you have any advice on how to deal with it?

A: Bear in mind that you would probably be just as worn down after facilitating an in-person event with 200 people. There are, however, a few differences, as well as potential solutions:

In person, we get live feedback from the people around us. We read their body language, hear them (hopefully) laugh at our jokes, and see when we are losing their attention. This is all much harder online. With larger groups, my best advice for this particular issue is to not use 'gallery view' and try to see everyone as tiny squares which can be quite stressful. Instead, use 'thumbnail view' if available which shows up to eight people. Also, try to look into the camera when you are speaking and not on the screen even though that's where the faces are!

Next, in person you would not be staring at your own face for an hour and a half, thinking about how your hair looks or how that pimple is really in the spotlight from your kitchen lamp. This is easily fixed by using the function to 'hide self-view'.

Lastly, whether in person or online, the power of a break cannot be underestimated. Make sure to build in short breaks and get people to stand up or move around a bit to get fresh energy. For your 1.5 hour session I would have a 5-minute break after half an hour, and another 3-minute break about 20 minutes from the end.

Q: Is there any difference between sitting on a bus scrolling on the phone, or reading a book or newspaper?

A: On the one hand these seem very similar: we are filling an otherwise empty, perhaps boring, moment with something that makes us feel good. But while reading a book has multiple health benefits such as improving brain connectivity, increasing our vocabulary, empowering our empathy, reducing stress, and much more, scrolling social media can instead have negative effects over time. The amount of information we go through while scrolling is massive and stimulates rather than relaxes.

Q: My 11-year-old daughter does not have her own smartphone yet and complains that all her friends are just on their devices during breaks at school, and sometimes even in class. We are reluctant to get her one but do not want her to feel left out. Any thoughts?

A: You are doing a great job actively considering what devices your daughter should have, and trying to guide her to the best of your knowledge. If you feel strongly about the position you have taken, I would suggest talking to the school, and other parents, or maybe the PTA. Overuse of social media and screen time regularly comes out as a top concern in parental polls so you are far from alone in your dilemma. Maybe you are just the parent who has managed to hold out the longest!

Schools are increasingly looking over device policies and I have met schools who have gone down different paths. Some simply have a no phone policy, while others have a compromise, e.g. students can bring it to school but hand it in to a teacher in the morning and get it back in the afternoon.

If that feels too overwhelming and you decide to get her a phone after all, I would suggest talking to her about her expectations, what she wants to use it for and how to best use it for her benefit, and of course safety. There is plenty of great material available for free online.

Lastly, remember that while this is really tricky, it is of course nothing new. When I grew up, I constantly tried to push boundaries by pointing to other kids who had certain toys, gadgets or a later curfew.

Q: **These practices seem great for adults but it's hard to follow your principles with a 17-year-old screaming in your face.**

A: First, have you changed your own habits already? My first advice is always to start with you; hopefully they will see the effort you are putting in and slowly start opening up to changed habits. The use of digital technology, and social media in particular, is like any other part of raising kids when they want something badly and we need to teach them to regulate it. Involve them as much as possible in the discussion. Be as collaborative as possible, but also be clear that screentime is a privilege, not a right. There are also great supportive resources online, some even made by teenagers for teenagers and parents.

Q: **I let my kids watch something on the iPad when I cook. Is that bad?**

A: If you do it every once in a while, then no. But if this becomes a necessity for you to be able to cook, then it is a problem and they miss out on vital moments to be bored, practice their self-regulation and imagination. Perhaps there is something that they can help with while cooking, something at their level? Another great trick is to have a box of toys that *only* comes out when adults need to cook or wash dishes or clean.

Q: **Are you against digital technology? Are you saying it was better in the days before it came?**

A: I am definitely not against technology. And as far as whether things were better before, I honestly do not know. But I definitely think it was *easier,* as the options were fewer. We are where we are, and it is not realistic to take steps back in our technical development. What *is,* however, both realistic and of utmost importance is to reflect on why we use any existing and new technology, what value it adds, how we can use it in the best way possible, what it is taking away, and how can we use it in a balanced way to get the good things out of it but avoid the detrimental effects.

APPENDIX:
OTHER VOICES

Excerpted from an interview with Teodora Pavkovic, Psychologist, Parenting Coach & Digital Wellness Expert

Q: **What is the interaction and link between teens' mental health and the use of social media?**

A: Some dramatic reporting by the Wall Street Journal in 2021 indicated that about one-third of teenage girls that were experiencing depression felt that it was the result of their usage of Instagram. So their experiences on Instagram were contributing to their depressed mood, and this was most likely the result of body comparisons and body issues. We know from this example, and many others, that interacting online and spending time in certain virtual spaces can cause distress and a deterioration of mental health. Also, some of the research shows that younger people who are already experiencing depression tend to spend more time interacting with the online world. Maybe to seek support, information, or for escapism. We know that there is a very, very powerful link between our mental health and wellbeing and the online world. But the causation can go both ways and it is important to be aware of this. Especially if you are a parent, and have a teenager who is using social media. There is a solid chance that their mental state could be made worse, or better, depending on how they use the particular social media platform. If they are able to find resources, follow people who have gone through their own struggles and have helpful insights and are supportive and compassionate, that can be wonderful. On the other hand, if most of what they are experiencing online is comparing themselves to influencers, coming across pornographic material, or experiencing cyberbullying (which we know is a significant issue for teens who are experiencing mental health issues), then you need to be more mindful of your teens' tech habits, have frequent conversations about them, and make sure that you have an insight into what they are doing, how they are doing it, how much and with whom.

Q: Many adults find it hard to have that conversation with teenagers. How can caregivers support and work with their teenagers on this?

A: In the U.S., there are now quite a few nonprofits exclusively focused on young people and their experiences with technology—many, like LookUp.Live, facilitate programs and events that encourage older teens and college students to speak to younger Gen Zers. I think that is a great way to do it, to encourage conversations between the generations, and to step away for a little bit as the adults in the room. I've also found that plenty of younger millennials and older Gen Zers have an awareness of the potential negative effects that technology can have—they are still aware of trends and pop culture, but are not 'hooked' to their devices. So even if parents find it difficult to have these conversations themselves, they can look to other young people for help. There is a huge benefit in getting young people to speak to each other.

One other thing I also always say to parents (and educators) is that it is too late to begin these conversations in middle school or high school. They need to begin well before, and the earlier they do the easier it will be to maintain them. You want to explore questions with your child around what it is going to look and feel like once they start using a particular social media or gaming platform, what will be the ins and outs of it, the positives and negatives. Start to think about strategies to address possible issues of excessive use or instances of cyberbullying, and help your child problem solve around how they can keep themselves safer and healthier online. Conversations, really, need to start at elementary school, but there are also ways we can discuss technology use even with children as young as kindergarteners.

Q: Is it too late if my teen is already using social media excessively?

A: It is never too late, even if in some ways you have arrived late at the party, so to speak. The positive side of kids already having used social media or different types of platforms, is that they have some experience of that already. There will be a lot of material there that you can use in your conversations.

One of the most important and encouraging things for parents to know, is that kids are not stupid! They are not as blind or as clueless as we often think. They know what the negative aspects are of this technology. But they will shut you down depending on how you approach them. If you approach them with the assumption that they know nothing and you actually have all the insights into what is good and bad, you will likely get shut down. It was the same with children and their parents in the 90s or 80s or 70s. That aspect of childhood and parenthood will never change, and it is not related to the technology we do or do not have.

So, if you are approaching a 16 year-old about this issue of technology use, you definitely don't want to approach them from the perspective that you know 'more' or 'better.' You also don't want to make assumptions about what they do or don't know already, or what they are thinking or feeling. The scary thing the statistics show us, is that the likelihood is high that the average 16 year-old has already come across pornography, cyberbullying, hate speech, and a whole bunch of other negative content and experiences online. Stats also show that they often don't want to share that they have been exposed to these things, because they fear that the adults' immediate reaction will be to take away the device or delete the app. In that situation, you will have to override your instinct to do that; go back and think: 'What am I trying to achieve here, what am I actually trying to help my child with, what is the end goal?'. The end goal is definitely not for the teen to shut down and storm out screaming at you. It is to have a conversation. At least to start having a conversation.

Q: How do I start a conversation with a teenager about their technology use?

A: Ask questions like, "What is the biggest misconception that you think that I have around your tech usage"; "What do you think are the things that I don't understand"; "What has your experience been like using TikTok, has it been mostly good or bad"; "What are the aspects of your tech use that you want to keep, and which ones do you want to change?"; " Do you see yourself using this app for another 5 years, or do you think you will grow tired of it?"; "Have you had any really bad experiences online?"; "Have you felt that you have needed to change your online behaviors, and how have you done that?"

They will likely have answers to all of these questions (especially if they are teens), but even if they don't yet, just keep in mind that this is not about disciplining your kids or catching them doing something bad, but about having a conversation and strengthening your relationship with them, so that when bad things happen to them on or offline they know that they can come to you.

Q: What else should I as a caregiver do?

A: I always go on about checking the age ratings—but it's really so important! Check the maturity and appropriateness levels of the content your child wants to engage with. You may hate having to do it, but it's important to take those 20 minutes to learn this.

Another piece of investigative research done by the WSJ showed just how quickly an algorithm (in this case, TikTok's) can take you down a rabbit hole of inappropriate or harmful content. An 8-year-old, for example, will not have the sufficient knowledge, insight or impulse control to not click on the next intriguing thing that pops up on a platform like TikTok. The challenge for parents today is that, in some cases, even that innocent video of cute dancing puppies could potentially lead the viewer to pornographic material (parents have shared stories of this happening with videos like Peppa Pig and Paw Patrol on You Tube, for example). Of course, a child can never unsee something like that, and you as a parent might find yourself in a situation where you will need to have a discussion about sex much earlier than you intended to. This is why we need to be focused on safeguarding them from an early age, and not only that, but teaching them how to safeguard themselves.

There is also no reason why you couldn't 'transplant' the same kinds of values you have as a family around 'offline' issues, like responsible drinking, to technology use. Parents don't always realize that the use of online platforms can be a lot more complicated than just simply watching fun videos of pets or people dancing—not every single social media user experiences its potential harms, but it is vital for parents to know what they are and how to lessen the chances of their children experiencing them.

Q: Do you think that the discussion about the negative effects of digital technology is exaggerated?

A: Every once in a while, I do get comments from people who think that I might be exaggerating the negative role that technology plays. There are also those who feel that the discussion, in general, is too alarmist. I strongly believe that everyone needs to have the opportunity to voice their own opinion about technology, so that we can have a conversation about it together and problem-solve together. The comforting news is that there are already organizations out there, like All Tech Is Human, who are doing this on a large scale.

. . . .

On the other hand, I don't think that by now—in 2022—there's anyone out there who thinks that the way modern-day technologies are built is entirely beneficial to us as individuals or as societies. We know that social media platforms are built in such a way that anger- and fear-inducing news spreads tens of times as fast as neutral or joyful news; we know that there is a multitude of easily-accessible websites and Facebook groups where people can quickly become radicalized; we know that digital media, because of the algorithms that support it, polarizes issues and decontextualizes them to the point where we end up with a very black-and-white outlook on reality; and we also know that both adults and children are constantly complaining about being distracted and feeling mentally scattered because of the sheer volume of information available online and the number of platforms through which this information is available. Let's also not forget about the thousands (possibly millions?) of parents around the world who are finding it genuinely hard to understand their digital natives and their online lives, and are therefore lacking in confidence when it comes to helping them stay safe online and develop digital citizenship skills.

The fascinating thing is that whether I speak to someone in the U.S., or Singapore, or the U.K., or my native Serbia, I always hear relatively similar stories, whether about the struggles of parenting in the age of technology, or the spread of misinformation, or the detrimental effect excessive technology use has on people's ability to focus.

Ultimately, the positive psychologist in me absolutely believes that we need to establish a balance through which we will continue to focus on and amplify everything that is good about technology, while continuing to seek out all the glitches that can make technology unsafe and damaging, especially to the youngest generations.

Learn more at www.teopcoaching.com.

Excerpted from an interview on traveling unplugged with Dr. Lena Waizenegger, Senior Lecturer at Auckland University of Technology, New Zealand

Our smartphone is a vital travel companion and amazingly handy with everything from keeping in touch with friends and family, sharing the photos of our trip on social media, to finding our way somewhere. Now imagine traveling without it. Terrifying thought? Up for the challenge?

. . . . .

Q: How did people feel before the digital detox travel study?

A: Some were anxious and nervous because nowadays we live as much in the digital world as the physical world and you are even more dependent on your smartphone when you are traveling, but others were quite excited because they were like "Oh, thank god, I can stop all my commitments for the moment."

Q: What were the "rules" of the study?

A: The requirement for the participants of the study was to travel without technology for at least one day during their travels. People had to go cold turkey, where you are fully disconnected. While this was the initial requirement, most of our participants still had their smartphone with them but didn't use the Internet, but some offline functions of the phone like the camera . . . Others switched to Do Not Disturb and just had emergency calls coming through.

Q: *What were the initial reactions?*

A: As soon as they digitally disconnected for a lot of them it was really a shock. There was almost a wake-up call, like, "Okay, we are just so reliant on technology in every facet of our life, but also in every facet of traveling". So we had some participants that arrived and they hadn't planned anything ahead of the trip. They were like, "Okay, how do we get to our hotel? How do we withdraw money?". All these rather simple things all of a sudden became a massive challenge, right? Therefore, they really had to find new ways and re-learn how to travel in a disconnected way. Others arrived at their destination and had a really big urge to get in contact with family and friends, because they were just so worried their family and friends couldn't reach them. And that created a lot of anxiety for them. So for a lot of our participants it was quite a shock to the system. And for others, especially for those who were better prepared, it was also a challenge, but they felt at ease much quicker, because they've printed out the maps, they have researched how they get to the accommodation, they have done some research on how to get around the city?

Q: What did they experience after the initial shock?

A: What we said is that 'we disconnect to reconnect'. We disconnect from technology to reconnect to nature and the people around us. This was kind of the tagline, really. And it's so true, because we had participants, they were so anxious to talk to other travelers to get directions or to inquire about new places to visit. We had one couple that literally negotiated about who is talking to one of the locals, right? Because they were like, "Oh, no, you do it! No, you do it!". And then they did and they found an amazing local beach which wasn't in any travel guide, only the locals knew. And then it was just such a wake-up call, because then they realized that there's just such a huge mass of local knowledge to tap into!

We had another couple that was traveling in Taipei who wanted to go to one of these famous templates, but they couldn't find it because they couldn't use any technology. So they were just walking through the alleys trying to find it, but on the way they found another, completely hidden temple. And there they met the ward at the entrance. And they sat down with him for an hour and he taught them everything around the temple and the religion. They got a secret tour, and little presents as well. And they would have never had these amazing experiences if they would have just gone straight to the tourist temple with Google maps! Now they found a temple that no one ever visits. It was also super special for the guy who took care of the temple, because he had two tourists coming in. And also for them, it was really special, because they got to know the locals, their religion, only because they were traveling without technology.

There are a lot of these much more rich experiences if you actually let go of control. As far as technology goes, we always want to be safe and be in control and know exactly where we go, or let someone know if we are five minutes late. But for those people who really jumped in the cold water and disconnected they had the most amazing experiences. And over time, they also realized this, and just became far less anxious and just went with it. 'So this is how it is now, we can't use any technology, we don't have access to the internet. And, you know, we just roll with it, right.' And so they learned how to navigate this in a disconnected way. They learned how to approach people.

Q: What was the most surprising finding?

A: I think the most interesting one was that afterwards, people just didn't want to connect again! You know, imagine, they were just so anxious right at the beginning. And, just, completely lost, right? And then they really had this massive development, this massive learning curve on so many Levels, especially personal. Another interesting finding was around reconnecting with your travel buddy. Because I think perhaps nowadays, you watch a movie on the plane, you know, then in the hostel, you're just on your phone, right? And when you are out and about you post content on social media. But if your travel is completely disconnected from technology you just talk much more, right. Especially for the couples, and we heard so often that, it was really, a long time since they had in-depth conversations, and like, through this digital disconnected time, they got so much closer again with each other, because they actually really listened to each other.

Q: What would you recommend for someone wanting to try this?

A: For the sake of reducing the stress on yourself and on, you know, your work, colleagues and friends and family I suggest doing it on the weekend or on holidays. Because there are fewer people trying to reach you.

And, you know, a lot of companies don't expect you to respond to emails.

Q: How do you try to keep a balanced technology use in your life?

A: So for me, distraction is a massive topic, which I totally try to circumvent. My phone is always on silent, I don't get any notifications, I don't get any email or social media notifications, because they distract me from focusing on my tasks. And my phone is always, you know, it's never on my desk, it's always tucked away. I use the Pomodoro Technique a lot for my work. So as soon as I realize I'm procrastinating or I distract myself, I just turn on a Pomodoro timer. These are pretty much the two things: trying to avoid any kind of distractions, and using the Pomodoro Technique, that's really effective.

I'm a massive fan of digital technologies. I think we just learn how to use them in a better way.

. . . . .

You can follow Lena and her work on LinkedIn: www. nz.linkedin.com/in/lenawaizenegger.

Excerpted from an interview with Hector Hughes, co-founder of Unplugged

Q: What is Unplugged?

A: We help busy city folk switch off by providing a digital detox at beautiful cabins an hour from city life.

Q: Why do you think people come to your cabins?

A: To destress, recharge, and reconnect with themselves.

Q: What is the feedback you get from guests? What outcome do they experience?

A: People tell us that when they book they see locking away the phones as a bit of a gimmick but after coming to stay that turns out to be the revelation.

Another great line we hear is that people realize the world doesn't end when they go offline. An important lesson!

Q: What is your own biggest challenge regarding tech-life balance?

A: The excitement of running a business. It's very difficult to switch off because I enjoy what I do. Yet, it's still so important. I really have to work at taking time off.

Q: Share your best advice/hack to support a healthy tech-life balance.

A: Going tech-free between 6 pm and 9 am. 15 hours offline each day does wonderful things to clear the mind. Most of us just don't need to be on our devices in the evenings and early mornings. Take a break.

Q: How do you see us using digital technology in 10 years?

A: Hopefully more mindfully. It's an incredibly difficult problem to solve but I'm a big believer in human ingenuity. I'm sure we'll figure it out.

Q: What is the best thing about digital technology?

A: It's empowering. It enables people in the poorest parts of the world to gain access to things we take for granted, like banking and a chance to earn from the digital economy. There's a long way to go but the possibilities are infinite.

Q: Do you have any other thoughts on tech-life balance?

A: The best way to predict the future is to build it. We might end up in a world where people do spend all day staring at screens or we might be able to create an alternate future. I'm hopeful for the latter.

. . . . .

See more at www.unplugged.rest!

Excerpted from an interview with Anna Tebelius Bodin, author and motivational speaker, Sweden

Q: What is "the sustainable brain"?

A: The sustainable brain takes actions that we can keep performing over time. It does not just make decisions based on the moment but supports the type of person we want to be long-term and makes us proud of the decisions we make.

Q: How does dopamine affect our brains?

A: Our brains are designed for the behaviors that helped our ancestors survive. Their attention was meant to be directed towards things that were surprising, new, and unexpected. These things gave us a dopamine hit and helped us survive.

Q: How has technology impacted our brains?

A: There is a massive difference between living today and living just 15 years ago. There are so many temptations, so much easily accessible dopamine. We live in an abundance and it is so much easier to consume now than 10–15 years ago. We consume because we can, not because it is good for us. We can constantly get new dopamine hits and we continue to consume not because it is fulfilling, but because it is increasingly more discomforting to stop.

Q: What is the risk with excessive dopamine from technology?

A: Everything we value as being worth something lies on the other side of discomfort, but we will never get there if we only stick to consumption that does not require an effort. We will not get over the hindrances to get to what matters, what really supports long-term wellbeing. Our consumption of information becomes a dopamine kick which brings on stress, and we supplement the stress with new stress.

Q: How can we make it easier to stop any unwanted behavior that feels good momentarily, like scrolling?

A: You can reduce the withdrawal for dopamine kicks by doing something stimulating that requires some form of effort, like socializing, reading, or exercising. The dopamine then increases slowly rather than becoming a kick. The difference between a kick and a slowly increasing level is the feeling afterward. After a two-hour football game, you are full of energy and motivation and can deal with "boring" tasks, but after two hours of scrolling, you probably feel drained.

If our whole life is dopamine hits, then everything else becomes a discomfort. Everything that is not an instant hit becomes uncomfortable and we teach the brain to crave these hits.

Q: Share your best advice/hack to support a healthy tech-life balance.

A: First of all, there is an important principle around behaviors. The problem that appeared in 2007 was not what we started doing, but what we *stopped* doing. It is not that you cannot scroll social media or watch Netflix or use your phone in the bathroom—just do what makes you feel good *when you look back at your choices*. Think about those things that you wish that you did. Think of yourself as someone who already does those things.

The next step demands the strength to make the right decisions when we have the choice. You do not get that strength by constantly giving into the easy option, but by doing those things that strengthen. One such exercise is to do two minutes of full silence. Don't consume anything.

How did you feel? The harder this is, the more you need it! The brain is made to think, not consume. Our current way of life—where we consume for the entire time we are awake time—has large consequences for our brain. If you can work your way up to 10 minutes of silence per day and do this for a month, you can actually see a physical change in a brain scan of the synapses after a month! You will have improved mental strength and neural network.

Q: How do you think our view of "attention-grabbing technology" will change in the next 10 years?

Everything goes in two directions, and there are extremes on both sides. On the one hand, more people are making themselves addicted by not making their own choices. There is a large group unaware of their digital consumption. This will become worse as technology becomes even more easily accessible. But then, on the other hand, there is a backlash—mainly driven by 25 to 45-year-olds, the generation that remembers life without the internet but grew up during its evolution. Institutions like schools need to work with this to raise awareness.

I think that the younger generation is wise and will have the driving force needed to make something really good out of themselves!

Excerpted from an interview with TJ Power, Mind Consultant and Founder of Digital Mind, The UK

Q: How is modern life affecting us? And why are we seeing these challenges now?

A: We've been in this kind of form for 200,000 years. So not actually altered that much. But our behavior has obviously hugely altered. We are pretty fundamentally designed to just be kind of very advanced animals wandering around and running around in forests, eating and sleeping, and breathing, and socializing and interconnecting with that kind of experience as a human, and you kind of take it to what life looks like now, which is more of a wake up in the morning, off goes the alarm on your phone, phone screen comes into the face, consuming a million different perspectives and thoughts and information and things that might stress you out, then you kind of go down, you might then spend 8–10 hours behind the computer in a day, spend the evening watching TV, and then like back onto the phone when you're lying in bed. And it's just like, the disparity between what a human actually was evolutionarily designed to do here. And what we're doing now is pretty different. And I think it is affecting our minds, our brains and thinking with what's going on here. I really think we undervalue how unique it is this century that we're all living in, because you've had humans for 200,000 years, say. I think many people would agree that in the next two to three to four decades, this tech is going to get very interconnected with us, maybe glasses and then moving kind of through their augmented reality and virtuality. And I really believe that we're living in this 100-year shift of 200,000 years in the past. We're in this gap, where we're in the merger with all of this tech and stuff. And I think it's a very unique time to be here and a time to really deeply understand what on earth is going on and try and use it all in the best way we can.

Q: You talk a lot about the brain and neurotransmitters, what is the deal there?

A: I've become very fascinated by these two neurotransmitters, dopamine. That's kind of the motivator, the one that gets us to do things, orientates our behavior in a certain direction. And then serotonin, the one that makes us feel good, the one that's made in our body that is responsible for our mood and sleep and all those kinds of things. And I think in modern life, we are stimulating our brain so much and activating this dopamine so much with our work and flicking off on our email and seeing if your business is doing well or going on social media and seeing what people are up to or putting stuff on social media. Then we have obviously all of the alcohol and the fast food and the online shopping. I think we've kind of begun to over-prioritize the mind and under-prioritize the body, which is having a big effect on how we feel.

When we experience dopamine naturally, it makes us feel awesome. If you think of a time you've gone out, and you've done a nice amount of exercise, and you've come home, you think you've got that real sense of accomplishment or say you decide to cook a meal and put 45 minutes into making a meal, and then you sit down and you eat it. And you get that real natural reinforcement from dopamine, where it makes you feel like, "Yes, this is something good that I've done." And that is what dopamine is designed to do. The challenge with dopamine is that we're supposed to earn it effectively, we're actually supposed to put in a certain amount of effort to be allowed to receive it. And that's how it managed to guide our behavior to help our survival. Now, obviously, we've been humans and short-circuited the putting-in effort part. So it's just straight to dopamine, straight dopamine, whether it's alcohol, or drugs, or fast food, or the phone, which is the number one source of dopamine, I think in society.

Q: What can we do about this?

A: One of my absolute missions with people in their relationship with tech is to do a daily dopamine detox for about 45 to 60 minutes a day. And that isn't actually that much time, it seems unusual to have to guide people to that. But most people don't really go 45–60 minutes in a day without either being on their computer or looking at their phone—it's normally just not that way.

So what I try and guide people to do is their first kind of step was beginning to find some kind of balance with tech is find a full hour in the day where they aren't on their phone, and they have to read or go and cook some food or go and socialize and have no screens, go out into nature go whatever it may be. But I'd say that step one is just every day finding a period of space where you go out and you earn your dopamine. And you could earn it by putting an effort into cooking, exercising, hanging out with people, whatever it may be. So your brain gets that natural experience rather than the artificial one that the phone provides.

Q: If 45–60 minutes sounds hard, how can someone ease into this?

A: Being phone-free as much as possible straight after waking up, when the brain is in a really vulnerable state. And also when socializing with friends, when you're outside in nature, and when you go to sleep.

Q: What's your own biggest challenge relating to technology?

A: Mine is definitely social media and seeing whether the things I create resonate with people because I love making this content. Like, I really love all of that kind of experience. And I obviously receive a hit of dopamine because, like, it's nice to try and succeed in life. I mean,

I have all those things turned off because there's chaos if I haven't. But I'll go and check it. And if I see a comment, and it says like this strategy really worked, like it gave me a boost in my head or whatever it may be, I'm like, "Yes, because I spent ages thinking about it." And now it's helping someone, however, so it's good, because I appreciate the fact that it's helping someone. But it can be addictive to see if the help is occurring. And that is probably the biggest thing I navigate, which means I use that scheduled summary thing on notification. Which only has you get notifications twice a day on my phone, which I find helps quite a lot. Yeah, that's my biggest challenge. And really, my only proper, proper way to get away from it is actually just get away from the flat. Like if it's near me. And I'm like, I don't know, cooking or something like it could be chat tempting to check on the phone. So I always try to leave it in other rooms or put it upstairs and put it on airplane mode. I try to actually physically create distance from it to give myself the space.

. . . . .

See more at www.instagram.com/tjpower/ or www. thedigitalmind.io.

Excerpted from an interview with Sohail Kashkari, Technology Discipline & Distractions Coach, Psychology B.Sc. (New Zealand)

Q: You have worked with people who spend up to 10 hours watching YouTube videos although they want to focus on other things. How do you help them?

A: A lot of people think it's about just trying harder, but we're kind of outgunned and don't have the tools. We have these media and tech companies that invest all their money into figuring out how they can influence us to spend as much time as possible using their technology. And essentially what I do is I teach the people who need those extra tools, how to take back control from those influences, and have more energy and capacity to reinvest into the areas that are important to them.

This can sometimes be simple as using tools such as newsfeed blockers and app limits. Or it can be slightly more complex by changing how we use the apps, such as how they appear, navigate and are accessed. This essentially makes them more 'boring', less easily accessible and less efficient at getting your clicks and taking your time. On a deeper level, this can also involve digging into how you think about your technology and the role it plays in your life. This can involve becoming more conscious of impacts of technology dynamics and distractions, its role on your psychology, and the impact it will have on your life over the long term.

Q: What is the most common problem that your clients have?

A: When does something become a problem? For example, if you smoke one single cigarette, you don't necessarily have any problems yet, but if you smoke cigarettes every day over time, there's a pretty high risk that you're going to get lung cancer. Then you've got a problem. To use Instagram as an example, there's actually a lot of evidence that Instagram can very quickly have detrimental effects on people's mental health. But when does it become a problem, right? Because even if you just use it for a short amount of time, you feel like you're fine. However, sometimes these effects can either compound over time or have subtler impacts. We don't necessarily recognize them quickly, but they can still be unhealthy behaviors even if we enjoy them. The people I work with often notice they have a problem when it starts really affecting the things that they care about in life. This can include their productivity at work, which can influence their ability to upskill, get promotions and get paid. It can influence their sleep, energy, and wellbeing, which can contribute to dynamics such as gaining weight and feeling bad about ourselves. It can also affect our relationships and connections to others we care about.

Q: What is your best technology hack?

A: I would say it's really all about becoming conscious of your intention for using your technologies, and finding ways to make it easier for yourself to stick with those intentions. Many people feel ashamed of their actions, and are not proud of binge-watching, scrolling for hours, and the like. This can perpetuate a negative cycle of unhealthy behavior where the shame and discomfort motivates us to reach for more distractions. I would invite people to explore making it easier for themselves, this really makes a huge difference. For example, most people have their cell phones set up optimized for distractions—with Facebook, TikTok and Instagram at the closest click of our fingers on our phones. If that is working for you, then great, but if you want to spend less time on these apps, then it's probably better that you move them somewhere else, or even try to delete them. So number one would be about getting really conscious of what you actually want from this app, what are you trying to achieve with it? Sometimes this can bring up deeper-seated problems that need to be addressed as well, which might require professional help to work through.

Q: Where do you think we will be in 10 years with this technology?

A: I think that we're already seeing huge movements in the right direction. There's a saying that I love which is that if you want to see the future, it is already here, it's just not distributed equally. In Silicon Valley, you can find a lot of people talking about how they actually don't let their kids use social media, or other technologies heavily. There's even some research on institutions like the Steiner and Montessori school systems where they delay the amount of time that they engage their children with digital technologies. The research found that the children actually ended up developing better academically, and creatively. Ultimately, this enables them to better use digital technologies. The point I want to highlight here is that the people who are well-informed in these areas, are often careful with how they their digital technologies.

Q: What are some experiences from your clients?

A: A common example is that people might be using YouTube for three or four hours a day, and want to do extra professional study to get a certification but they just keep watching YouTube instead and don't have the energy. After they start to develop extra tools from working together, they are able to manage their information consumption more consciously. They can complete their certification finally, get a huge pay raise, and then they're able to have all these extra benefits like sleeping better, feeling more relaxed, feeling proud of themselves for the work that they're putting in and going in the direction they want to go, rather than feeling like they're stuck in the mud, doing activities that make them feel less great about themselves.

Q: You were a big part of organizing Phone Free Day 2021. How was that?

A: It was a beautiful experience where we tried to help develop a counterculture where we are challenging people to go some time without using their phones. Our goal was just to raise awareness of giving it a go. But we got great feedback from people having an amazing time and saying, "What the heck, I couldn't believe that this was this good!". It was wonderfully overwhelming. Now I've had countless people tell me that they have permanently changed their habits just from this one experience of trying it. Yet there is so much opportunity still for us to define a healthy culture of digital technology usage. If you are trying to police your kids and tell them that they can only play one hour of video games, they will still try find other ways to get around this. or get screentime from other sources. So I'd like us to think more about how we can develop a culture of healthy and sustainable usage, one that we can work on collectively. Events like Phone Free Day really show us that there is a huge appetite for this and I think that is a really exciting direction moving forwards.

RESOURCES

THERE IS PLENTY OF LITERATURE THAT HOMES in on specific parts of tech-life balance and digital wellbeing. There are also many organizations that do amazing work educating and supporting this transition. While it is impossible to list all, here are a few to start with!

Common Sense Media
www.commonsensemedia.org
Nonprofit organization providing expert reviews, objective advice, helpful tools, and a lot more about kids and technology.

Center for Humane Technology
www.humanetech.com
A nonprofit organization working to educate about the attention economy and drive a shift toward technology that supports wellbeing and democracy.

Healthy Screen Habits

www.healthyscreenhabits.org

Nonprofit that educates and empowers families to create heathy habits for screen use.

Non-tech activities for kids

www.mothermag. com/100-screen-free-things-to-do-with-kids-at-home/

Online Pomodoro timer for timer

www.pomofocus.io

The News Literacy Project 10 questions for fake news:

www.courts.ca.gov/documents/BTB24-PreCon2G-3.pdf

Sensible Screen Use

www.sensiblesreenuse.org

Non-profit developed by health professionals that informs parents and teachers about impacts of tech and how to use it more purposefully.

FURTHER READING

Atomic Habits, James Clear (topic: building and breaking habits)

Scroll Zombies, Sven Rollenhagen (topic: social media)

How to Break Up With Your Phone, Catherine Price (topic: smartphones)

OFF. Your Digital Detox for a Better Life, Tanya Goodin (topic: general digital balance)

Stop Reading The News, Rolf Dobelli (topic: news and information overflow)

Deep Work, Cal Newport (topic: focus and productivity)

Indistractible, Nir Eyal (topic: focus and productivity)

Screen Kids: 5 Relational Skills Every Child Needs in a Tech-Driven World, Arlene Pellicane and Gary Chapman (topic: Technology and kids)

Creating a Tech-Healthy Family, Andrea Davis (topic: Technology and kids)

Ten Arguments For Deleting Your Social Media Accounts Right Now, Jaron Lanier (topic: social media)

ABOUT THE
AUTHOR

Taíno Bendz started Phone Free Day after realizing firsthand how technology can stress us out, get in the way of relationships, and even distract us from what's important in life. Through this non-profit initiative and his speaking business, his message about tech-life balance has reached and inspired hundreds of thousands of people around the world.

Taíno conducts research on digital technology usage, holds a master's degree in Engineering and Management and has spent the last ten years working in technology sectors such as renewable energy, healthcare IT, and software automation.

He currently lives in Sweden with his partner and two young sons, and enjoys being in nature, yoga, and pretty much all sports. For more information, visit **www.tainobendz.com**.